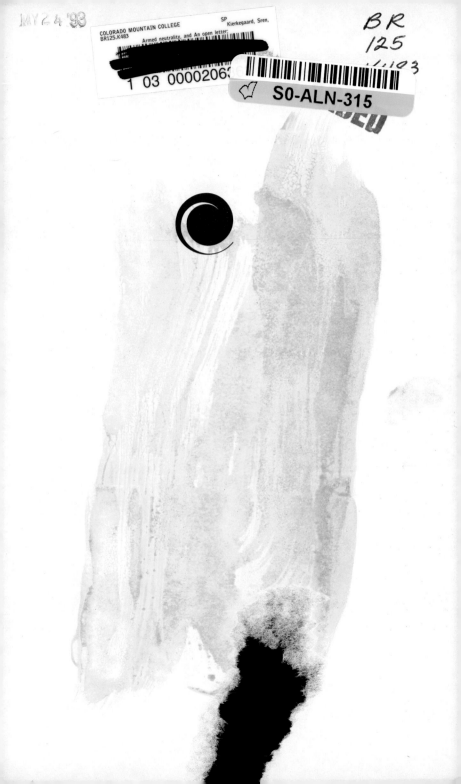

Søren Kierkegaard

ARMED NEUTRALITY
and
AN OPEN LETTER

WITH RELEVANT SELECTIONS FROM HIS
JOURNALS AND PAPERS

EDITED AND TRANSLATED WITH
AN INTRODUCTION BY
Howard V. Hong and Edna H. Hong

BACKGROUND ESSAY AND
COMMENTARY BY
Gregor Malantschuk

A CLARION BOOK
Published by Simon and Schuster

A Clarion Book
Published by Simon and Schuster
Rockefeller Center, 630 Fifth Avenue
New York, New York 10020
All rights reserved
including the right of reproduction
in whole or in part in any form
Copyright © 1968 by Howard V. Hong
Reprinted by arrangement with the Indiana University Press

FIRST PAPERBACK PRINTING 1969

SBN 671-20379-7

Manufactured in the United States of America
by The Murray Printing Co., Forge Village, Mass.

ACKNOWLEDGMENTS

The editors are indebted to Dr. Gregor Malantschuk for his share in this volume, through provision of the background essay "Søren Kierkegaard—Poet or Pastor?" and the Commentary on *Armed Neutrality* and *An Open Letter,* and through his observations on particular points and on the entire plan.

Acknowledgment is made to Lohses Forlag for permission to use Gregor Malantschuk's commentary on *Armed Neutrality,* which originally appeared in the first Danish edition, *Den bevæbnede Neutralitet* (1965), to Gyldendals Forlag for permission to absorb the notes on the *Papirer* and *Værker* in our annotation of the two texts, and to Rask-Ørsted Fondet for its support.

We gratefully acknowledge also the hidden contribution of Mary Petersen in the typing of the manuscript and of Catherine Brown in seeing the manuscript through the various stages of publication.

CONTENTS

ARMED
NEUTRALITY
and
AN OPEN
LETTER

Gregor Malantschuk

SØREN KIERKEGAARD— POET OR PASTOR?

The Conflict Behind
Søren Kierkegaard's Work
as an Author

Søren Kierkegaard's work as a writer can be considered and already has been considered from many different points of view, but as far as I know the conflict which lay behind this activity, a conflict between his felt need for poetic development and his constantly recurring desire to become a village pastor, has not yet been treated, in fact, has hardly been noticed.[1] In the following pages I shall briefly attempt to describe the background of this conflict, which is discussed only in his journals, and to sketch its progress through the succession of his works.

As will become apparent, it was precisely the tension between these two possibilities—pastor or poet—which goaded him to find the best way to serve Christianity and which thereby gave his work as an author its distinct originality, something he himself was aware of and expressed in the following words: "Now they can do with me what they will—insult me, envy me, stop reading me, bash in my hat, bash in my head, but they cannot in all eternity deny what was my idea and my life, that it was one of the most original thoughts for a long time, and the most original thought in the Danish language—that Christianity needed a maieutic, and I understood how to be that, although no one understood how to appreciate it."[2]

Kierkegaard developed his literary activity mainly along three parallel lines: his journal entries, the works under his own name, and pseudonymous writings. Since the journals are extremely important in the illumination of our theme, we will briefly state their place in the structure of his work as a writer.

In his journals alone Kierkegaard has created something completely unique and original, and these entries began a few years before his public appearance as a writer and continued until his death. This was Kierkegaard's hidden authorship, of which none of his contemporaries had an inkling. I know of no author who with the same consistency has created an entire hidden production which was to appear only after his death.

Kierkegaard regarded these entries in the journals as a useful preparation for the public literary activity itself. Most of the entries are written in an aphoristic style. They fit into P. M. Møller's characterization of his *Strøtanker (Random Thoughts)*: "Random thoughts, the fruit of the moment's more clear intuition, are poetic in their aphoristic form, not scholarly. They are the culmination points of thinking."[3] In his journals Kierkegaard gathered an enormous reservoir of such "culmination points of thinking" relating to the themes with which he was working; some of these thoughts he used later in his public literary activity, and others were left behind as an inexhaustible source of impulses which can lead us to think through man's most central and burning questions. Kierkegaard was himself clear about the significance of his journal entries, and he kept his diaries quite consciously with a view to posthumous publication. At one point he wrote of these entries: "Much of what I have even carelessly jotted in the journals will come to have great significance and influence."[4]

In these journals Kierkegaard also carried on a steady dialogue with himself concerning his personal problems. It is these particular entries which are most pertinent to our investigation. Without them we would not at all suspect how penetrating the conflict between the poet and the pastor was in Kierkegaard's life. If we wish to look at Kierkegaard's public activity as a writer from the point of view of this conflict, it is necessary to pay attention to the great number of journal entries which touch upon it.

Kierkegaard's first two works, published under his own name, were not yet affected by the question: poet or pastor. The first, *From the Papers of One Still Living*, 1838, was published before Kierkegaard began his final theological studies in earnest. The problem had not yet cropped up. Nor could the problem "poet or pastor" become acute in the other work, his doctoral thesis, *The Concept of Irony*, which came out approximately a year after he had taken his final theological examination. The author of *The Concept of Irony* did not regard himself as a poet; his doctoral dissertation was faithful to scholarly form and showed how thoroughly the author had entered into certain particular areas of a philosophical-theological nature.

The problem "poet or pastor" first appeared in the work which marked the beginning of Kierkegaard's real authorship, namely *Either/Or*, 1843. As Kierkegaard himself expressly wrote in many places, his unhappy engagement experience with Regine Olsen made him a poet. To communicate his feelings about it both to his contemporaries and first and foremost to Regine he had to use a poetic mode and pseudonyms.

Kierkegaard became a poet who had enough ideas in his back pocket for an enormous literary productivity. This great productivity was further advanced by a personal factor, which Kierkegaard described as follows: "When I left her, I chose death—for that very reason I have been able to work so enormously."[5]

Kierkegaard later asserted that while working on *Either/Or* he was already thinking of seeking a pastoral appointment right after the publication of the book. After this the thought of becoming a rural pastor recurred again and again, although with different motivation, as many of the entries in the journals indicate. The fact that Kierkegaard constantly mulled over the possibility of becoming a pastor could signify that he felt an obligation to his father. There is much evidence which seems to confirm this supposition. In 1835 Kierkegaard wrote as follows to his brother-in-law Peter W. Lund about his father's wish that he study theology: "As far as little annoyances are concerned, I will only say that I am starting to study for the theological examination, a pursuit which does not interest me in the least and which therefore does not get done so very fast. I have always preferred free, perhaps therefore also indefinite, studying to the boardinghouse where one knows beforehand who the guests will be and what food will be served each day of the week. Since it is, however, a requirement, and one scarcely gets permission to enter into the scholarly pastures without being branded, and since in view of my present state of mind I regard it as advantageous, plus the fact that I know by going through with it I can make father very happy (he thinks that the real land of Canaan lies on the other side of the theological diploma, but in addition, like Moses of old, ascends Mount Tabor and declares that I can never get in—yet I hope that it will not be fulfilled this time), so I'd better dig in."[6]

But that very year Kierkegaard nevertheless gave up his theological studies and did not resume them until after his father's death the summer of 1838. Troels-Lund in his book *Bakkehus og Solbjerg (Hill House and Sun Mountain)* speaks of this with these cryptic words: "This abandonment of theological studies must have affected the father deeply. The son's preparation to be a pastor was, to be sure, the son-sacrifice he had promised to bring to God."[7]

Concerning Kierkegaard's resolve after his father's death to finish his theological studies, Hans Brøchner states: "He told me that his father had always wanted him to take the theological examination and that they had discussed the matter very frequently. 'As long as father lived, I could defend my thesis that I ought not take it, but when he was dead and I had to take over his part in the debate, I could no longer hold my own and had to resolve to study for the examination.' "[8] In all probability when Bishop Mynster wanted Kierkegaard "out in the country" it was because of conversations he had previously had with the elder Kierkegaard and not simply because he regarded Kierkegaard as "a suspicious and even dangerous person."[9] It is reasonable to suppose that since Kierkegaard's father wished him to take the theological examination he expected him subsequently to seek a pastoral appointment.

But however this may be, Kierkegaard affirmed that he had already been mulling over the thought of seeking a pastoral appointment after the publication of *Either/Or*. This is found in many passages in his journals.

The earliest entry stating that after the publication of *Either/Or* Kierkegaard wanted to seek a pastoral appointment is from the year 1847, consequently four years after *Either/Or*. "They saw in me a man who aspired to become the public's most highly honored, cultured darling, to receive applause and become the genius of the age on parade. They were mistaken. They did not see in the first line I wrote that I was a preacher of repentance."[10] Later he added: "It was not evident, nor was it my thought at the time, but my thought was to become a pastor."[11] Here the thought of becoming a pastor is mentioned in direct connection with the time around the publishing of *Either/Or*.

A further confirmation that Kierkegaard had such early thoughts of seeking a pastoral appointment is found in some entries from 1845. In these notes Kierkegaard entertains the possibility of seeking a pastoral appointment but mentions as hindrance a hidden guilt. He wrote: "It was perhaps right to make a psychological experiment but at another point: a prospective clergyman, for example, who fears to become a clergyman (because of a guilt situation he goes to a remote place, because he does not dare do this at home for fear of being surprised, and reads canon law to see which sins are forbidden by the Church—*de occultis non judicat ecclesia*), and yet his only wish is to become a clergyman, because it seems to him to be the only way possible to make some compensation for his sin.—The dialectical contradiction between whether he is benefiting others by being silent about his sin and seeking to be effective in a more quiet manner or whether it would be better to divulge everything."[12] And further: "I have bought a new copy of canon law to study it again to see whether I again dare be a pastor—but just buying the copy makes me shudder, because it is as if the book dealer might notice on me what a painful study I am making of it."[13]

At that time he was already on the poetic path, and as poet he confessed of himself: "His suffering is that he continually wants to be a religious individual and continually goes wrong and becomes a poet: consequently an unhappy love affair with God."[14]

The entries cited above, which also point backwards in time, point to the period around the publication of *Either/Or*.

The contents of these entries make it highly probable that Kierkegaard was right when he later repeatedly declared that while writing *Either/Or* he already entertained the thought of becoming a pastor. It is also important to note that the motivation for his desire to become a pastor, which he expressed in 1845, coincides completely with other later statements about why he wanted specifically to choose the ministry about the time of the publication of *Either/Or*. In all these entries penitence is given as the motive.

An additional confirmation of Kierkegaard's early consideration of becoming a pastor is Pastor Villads Christensen's point in his book *Søren Kierkegaard*.[15] About a year after the publication of *Either/Or* Kierkegaard took the examination in homiletics and gave his terminal sermon. It could not be said more clearly that he was serious about seeking a pastoral appointment.

But then there is the question why Kierkegaard did not carry out his intention to seek a pastoral appointment after he had published *Either/Or*. The following entry from 1848 may be cited in answer: "It was my plan, immediately after the publication of *Either/Or* to seek a call in a village and sorrow over my sins. I could not force my productivity back, I followed it—naturally it now went into the religious."[16] In an entry from 1853 he discusses the matter in more detail: "When I left 'her' I begged one thing of God, that I might succeed in writing and finishing *Either/Or* (this was for her sake as well, for 'The Diary of a Seducer' was indeed intended to alienate her, or, as *Fear and Trembling* puts it: 'When the baby is to be weaned, the mother blackens her breast')—and then out to a parsonage. I considered this an expression for renouncing the world.

"The part about *Either/Or* succeeded. What happened then was not what I had expected and intended—that I would become hated, loathed, etc.—oh, no, I was a brilliant success.

"Consequently the wish, my request to finish *Either/Or*, was fulfilled.

"Now I should have been off to a parsonage as a country pastor. I owe it to the truth to admit that after such an enormous productivity in so short a time, after the sensation it created here at home, the thought somewhat left my mind. Moreover, there had awakened in me such an intense productivity I was unable to resist it.

"Consequently something else happened here—I became an author, but turned in the direction of becoming a religious author."[17]

Concerning his continuing activity as a writer, Kierkegaard explains in many other passages that inasmuch as he could not check his urge to write, the fact that he did not become a pastor had to show itself in a religious side or parallel series in the authorship. He did not become a pastor, but he could write edifying works. This is expressed very clearly in the following entry: "My first thought was to stop with *Either/Or*—and then straight to the rural parish. Since it did not happen, there was at once a religious signal (*Two Edifying Discourses*)."[18]

To this information it must be added that already in *Either/Or*, in the so-called "Ultimatum," at the end of Volume II, Kierkegaard had presented an edifying discourse. Curiously enough, the discourse is attributed to a pastor who had been "placed in a little parish on the Jutland heath."[19] Was it the father's wish, perhaps, that the son return as a pastor to his father's native soil?

It was, however, with the *Two Edifying Discourses*, published in May, 1843, that Kierkegaard began the independent series of edifying or upbuilding discourses which he brought out under his own name. With respect to the literary activity immediately fol-

lowing, in all probability Kierkegaard, while still working with
Either/Or, had worked out a larger plan of writing, encompassing
all the themes he treated in the works which were published the
following years, with *Concluding Unscientific Postscript* as the
last. Therefore the thought of giving up his writing had to retreat
steadily until the plan was completed. The journals give the following short description of the struggle between the poet and the
pastor during the period between the publication of *Two Edifying
Discourses* in 1843 and *Concluding Unscientific Postscript* in 1846:
"Soon, however, that other thought (a village pastor) came up
again. I intended to conclude as an author in the shortest possible
time—and then to the village parish.

"With each new book I always thought—now you must stop.
I felt it most clearly with *Concluding Unscientific Postscript*.

"Here it was my thought to stop—and then I wrote the lines
about *The Corsair*."[20]

After the publication of *Either/Or*, Kierkegaard continued his
authorship under the inner tension between two possibilities.
There were two lines of direction, corresponding to his two con-
tending tendencies, according to which he developed his authorship. In connection with *Either/Or* he created new works with
pseudonymous authors, and in these he regarded himself as a poet
with his center of gravity in esthetic territory. Beginning with *Two
Edifying Discourses* in May 1843 he continued with the parallel
edifying religious series, which for him took the place of work as a
clergyman.

As poet, Kierkegaard created first and foremost the works which
he said were written with Regine in mind. By Kierkegaard's own
statement this was the case with such of the esthetic works as
Either/Or, *Repetition*, and *Fear and Trembling*, but it must not
be forgotten that most of *Stages on Life's Way* originated in Kierkegaard's reflection on his relationship to Regine, especially over
the unhappy conclusion of the relationship. It must be added,
however, that because of the great wealth of universally human

existential experience, the works which contain a "hint" to Regine obviously have substance also for others.

In addition to the pseudonymous works mentioned above, in which Kierkegaard is a poet in the proper sense, he published during the first period of his authorship three other works in which the psychological or philosophical treatment of the themes is dominant: *The Concept of Anxiety* [Dread], *Philosophical Fragments*, and *Concluding Unscientific Postscript*.

As we have already seen from several of Kierkegaard's journal entries, it was his earnest determination to break off his writing activity after *Concluding Unscientific Postscript*. But this was precisely the time that the "*Corsair* affair" began. Looking more closely at the situation at the time, we discover that completely new factors, all of which contributed to making the choice between poet and pastor a more complicated matter, entered into the picture.

These factors are the following:

1. The effects of Kierkegaard's challenge to *The Corsair*.
2. Kierkegaard's new vision of his task as poet.
3. The beginning of a critique of the clergy and of the pastoral appointment as a means of making a living.
4. Kierkegaard's apprehensions about his future economic situation.

These new circumstances, each in its way, strongly influenced Kierkegaard's attitude toward the two possibilities, poet—pastor, and the previous clarity of the choice of alternatives was lost.

Before we go further into these four factors, we must consider the time around the publication of *Concluding Unscientific Postscript*. Even ten days before this work came out, Kierkegaard seems to have been completely sure that he would seek a pastoral appointment. February 7, 1846, he wrote: "My idea now is to qualify myself to become a pastor. For several months I have prayed God to help me proceed, for it has been clear to me for some time that I ought not be an author any more. I want to be altogether an author or not at all. For this reason I have not begun anything new while reading proof, except the little review of *The Two Ages*, which is my last work."[21]

But in a journal entry written a few days after *Concluding Unscientific Postscript* came out, a certain doubt about the choice of ministry is detectable. "If I only could make myself become a pastor. Out there in quiet activity, permitting myself a little productivity in my free time, I shall breathe easier, however much my present life has gratified me."[22]

In the beginning of the same entry it appears that Kierkegaard had a certain satisfaction about his position as an author after having published *Concluding Unscientific Postscript*. "*Concluding Unscientific Postscript* is out. The responsibility for the pseudonymity has been acknowledged. One of these days the printing of *A Literary Review* [*En literair Anmeldelse*] will begin. Everything is in order. I merely have to keep calm and quiet, confident that *The Corsair* will support the whole undertaking negatively just as I wish it. At the moment, as far as the plan is concerned, I am as correctly situated in literature as possible and also in such a way that it becomes a task to be an author. In itself it was the most propitious idea, the very moment I was finished with my authorship and by assuming all the pseudonyms ran the risk of becoming a kind of authority, that I then broke with *The Corsair* in order to prevent all direct overtures."

From the remarks just quoted we get the definite impression that Kierkegaard was clear that he was standing at the time in a situation of transition in which he was not completely sure what position he should take with regard to the choice between poet and pastor.

But soon the four factors previously mentioned began to make themselves felt and to exert their influence upon his reflections. We shall now examine them more closely.

1. Kierkegaard's challenge to *The Corsair* had the following effect:

   a. Kierkegaard considered that by challenging *The Corsair* he had ventured beyond the boundary of the poetic; he had come into direct contact with actuality or, as he expressed it: ". . . it becomes an act to be an author."[23] For Kierkegaard this meant that from now on he could permit himself to think of himself as more than a poet. From this time on, the occasional references in the journals to his being more than a poet simultaneously include allusions to his challenge to *The Corsair*. An example of such a remark is the following: "I am to this extent a little more than a poet, because I have had the courage to dare to expose myself to derision and to endure it."[24] Kierkegaard pondered further whether and how in the future he could play the part of "author in character"[25] as he termed it.

b. In another way the challenge to *The Corsair* and the subsequent conflict became significant for Kierkegaard by providing existential experience and teaching him that he who ventures something for the sake of truth will come to suffer. From this he concluded the principle (which is treated specifically in the essay "Has a Man the Right to Let Himself Be Put to Death for the Truth?")[26] that it is the individual himself and not the environment which determines the extent to which the individual is exposed to scorn and martyrdom. These thoughts subsequently played an important role as he reflected upon how far he dared to expose himself to suffering from the world about him.

Already the feeling of being an "author in character" as well as thoughts of voluntary suffering must have had a restrictive influence on Kierkegaard's wish to become a pastor.

c. Still more restrictive in this way was Kierkegaard's conviction that if he sought a pastoral appointment in the country after he had been exposed to violent attack from *The Corsair* this would be regarded as flight.

Consequently the effect of *The Corsair*'s attack upon him was that his plans for a pastoral appointment had to be set aside for the time being. This is expressed in the following note from about a year after he challenged *The Corsair*: "God be praised that I was subjected to the attack of wholesale vulgarity. I have now had proper time to learn inwardly and become convinced that there was something morbid about wanting to live out in a country parish in order to do penance in oblivion in an out-of-the-way place. I am more determined than ever before to stay where I am. If I had not experienced the deluge of mockery, I would always have been pursued by that melancholy thought, for a certain kind of prosperity encourages melancholy ideas. . . ."[27]

d. In the entry just quoted Kierkegaard mentions one more result of the mockery to which he was subjected by *The Corsair,* namely that he "has now had proper time to learn inwardly. . . ." This must be understood as an intimation that *The Corsair*'s attack had caused him to concentrate upon the edifying aspect of Christianity and thus had provided the push toward a stronger emphasis upon the purely Christian tone in his writing, as exemplified by *Edifying Discourses in Various Spirits, Works of Love,* and *Christian Discourses.*

All this must be said to be related to the first factor: the results of Kierkegaard's challenge to *The Corsair.*

2. The next factor was Kierkegaard's widening vision of the poet and his task, a vision which came to play a decisive role in his writing after the publication of *Concluding Unscientific Postscript.* This factor was closely related to Kierkegaard's thought of wanting to be more than a poet and to his concentration upon the edifying side of Christianity, occasioned by *The Corsair*'s attack. But the new view of the poet must be understood primarily from within, as part of the development Kierkegaard as author had to go through.

The center of gravity of Kierkegaard's activity as a writer until *Concluding Unscientific Postscript* lay within the esthetic and the universally human, the two domains proper to the poet. From Kierkegaard's point of view, the poet can also be characterized as a priest of the universally human.[28]

After the publication of *Concluding Unscientific Postscript* Kierkegaard had virtually exhausted the possibilities in the area of the human. If he was to continue as a writer, the center of gravity, quite consistently, must now move from the esthetic and the human to the religious. The poet must shift his position and become a religious poet.

Before discussing this new position it is appropriate to introduce here Kierkegaard's definition of a poet, a definition which in a wider sense also applies to the poet on the religious level. "What is it to be a poet? It is to have one's own personal life, his actuality, in wholly different categories than those of the poetic production, it is to relate oneself to the ideal merely in imagination, so that one's own personal existence is more or less a satire on the poetic production and on oneself. This is true of all the modern thinkers, too, even of the outstanding poets (I mean the German poets, for there are no Danish poets). On the whole life gets no higher than this. Most men live without idea. There are a few who relate poetically to the ideal but deny it in their personal lives."29

By Kierkegaard's own declaration, his becoming a poet of both the human and the religious came about because he had always placed actuality in relation to the highest ethical and religious ideals. This is explicated in the following entry, which refers to both forms of his poetic activity: "It was indeed my ideal to become a married man and make that my whole life. And then, despairing of achieving that, I became an author and perhaps a first-rate one at that. My next ideal was to become a village pastor, to live in a quiet rural setting, to become a genuine part of the little circle around me—and then when I despaired of that, it became possible for me to realize something which seems to be far greater."30

The despair was rooted in the fact that Kierkegaard applied a high criterion to life, as expressed in the following words: "My misfortune or that which makes my life so difficult is that I am strung a key higher than other men, and wherever I am, what I am doing is not preoccupied with the particular but always also with a principle and idea. Most people think at most about which girl they should marry. I have to think about marriage. So it is in everything.

"My situation at present is basically this. Most people think most of all about which appointment or office they should seek; but I am well within the whole struggle, this battle of ideas, this question of principle, to what extent so-called Christian offices are legitimately Christian."[31]

What Kierkegaard called the "question of principle" or in a wider sense the advancement of high ideals made it necessary for him to be satisfied on the human level with an unhappy relationship to the woman he loved. His insistence on the ideal as the only right standard for life—or marriage—did not permit him to bind himself to her, even though he knew very well that "many a [generally good] marriage harbors petty episodes."[32] In relation to the purely human, he had to be satisfied with becoming a poet.

The same relationship was repeated on a higher level. Kierkegaard took God's claim so seriously that, as he wrote as early as 1845, he suffered from "an unhappy love-affair with God."[33]

Consequently, because Kierkegaard could not realize the universal, and because he could not fulfill the claim he placed upon being a Christian, he became "an unhappy lover" in relation to Christianity and thereby a religious poet. Kierkegaard subsequently presented this latter conflict with special clarity in *The Sickness unto Death,* from which only a few quotations are given here. Kierkegaard calls a "poet-existence" characterized by the conflict just mentioned "the most eminent poet-existence," with which one has to agree if one thinks of Kierkegaard himself. His principal charge against this kind of poet is that he poetizes "the good and the true" "instead of being that—that is, existentially striving to be that." This quite clearly reflects Kierkegaard's own battle between poetizing and acting, which is apparent in many journal entries around 1846. Moreover, Anti-Climacus-Kierkegaard discusses the two kinds of unhappy loves, the one on the human level, the other on a higher level, which create the two above-mentioned types of poets. This refers primarily to Kierkegaard himself. Of the religious poet's connection to the human we read: "Just as someone who became unhappy in love and thereby became a poet blissfully praises the happiness of love, so also he becomes the poet of the religious life." Further: "But just as that poet's description of love, so this poet's description of the religious life has a fascination, a lyrical swing which no married man and no His Reverence can effect."[34]

Kierkegaard understood that his task as a religious poet was to present increasingly rigorous claims—thus this factor, too, was unable to encourage his resolve to seek a pastoral appointment.

3. The third factor, which also emerged shortly after *Concluding Unscientific Postscript* was published, was Kierkegaard's constantly stronger charges against the clergy, that they were primarily interested in their "bread and butter." One of the first entries about this reads: "As a rule the 'bread and butter' consideration plays a decisive role in the world; wherever this middle term drops out, men become irresolute. The Christians in name only, who actually have no impression of the essentially Christian, do not disapprove at all that a clergyman recites the orthodox doctrine, and why not? Because it is his bread and butter. They make no objection at all that the preacher in his sermon advances strong claims upon life, and why not? It is part and parcel of his trade, just as a military officer looks stern and a police officer strikes. When, however, a private man is religious in a stricter sense and expresses his religiousness, he is regarded as mad. And why? Because the bread-and-butter middle term is lacking."[35]

With this entry, in which Kierkegaard is still relatively mild in his judgment of the clergy, began a long series of denunciations culminating in the Church battle.

The question naturally arises: how could Kierkegaard think of a pastoral appointment after beginning to conduct a steadily stronger critique of the ministry? Kierkegaard believed the problem could be solved by simply admitting that he was not better than other pastors and that he was seeking the pastoral appointment for economic reasons. "Of course I have absolutely nothing to say against a man's working for a living and the like; I aim to do it myself; but it must be clear that this is not in order to serve the truth. The truth does not require that I become a high-ranking, distinguished man and the like; it makes no difference at all to the truth whether I live on dry bread—consequently it cannot be for the sake of the truth. That it is supposed to be, as is said, to accomplish more with the help of one's position—this makes a mockery of Christ and all witnesses of the truth, who alone have shown how one accomplishes the most for the truth. If, however, I want to have this high-ranking position—well, but then one admission—that it is for my own sake."[36]

4. We now come to the fourth factor, Kierkegaard's incipient apprehension about his future economic situation. This factor, too, appeared shortly after the publication of *Concluding Unscientific Postscript*. Before that time, as has been shown, it was penitence which motivated his desire to go out to the country as a pastor; now it was mainly economic insecurity which prompted him. This is apparent in the many journal entries in which Kierkegaard's concern about his future economic situation is put into words. The presence of the hindering factors previously named meant that he had to battle simultaneously with misgivings about seeking an appointment and with his economic concern.

To put an end to the repeated reflections on this matter and to reassure himself that he finally for once had attempted to obtain an appointment, he resolved in June 1849 to seek out J. N. Madvig, the cabinet secretary for ecclesiastical and educational affairs, as well as Bishop Mynster. Kierkegaard wrote about this under the heading, "A Historical Notation": "In order to satisfy myself that it *is not* because I am reluctant to make a step in the opposite direction, the day before yesterday (Saturday) (after I failed to meet Mynster on Friday) I was at Madvig's but did not meet him. That was probably fortunate. For I dare say in my own defense that this time, as usual, I intended to take this step, but always with the possibility of gaining impetus to act in the very opposite direction; this is something peculiar to my nature, because what tempts me as possibility, when it appears capable of becoming actuality becomes something else for me."[37] What is meant is clarified in the following appended note: "Yes, it is true. Would to God they had offered me an appointment; then it would surely become far easier for me to understand that I could not undertake it. But here comes the self-tormenting in me again; when it is not offered to me, then I am afraid that the reason I do not take the necessary step is that I am being soft with myself."[38]

A few days later Kierkegaard went to Mynster again, but since Mynster did not have time they did not discuss the matter.

Kierkegaard actually felt relieved after this unproductive attempt; now he had done something from his side; he even reproached himself for possibly having already ventured too far out.[39] We can say that with this attempt Kierkegaard's interest for a pastoral appointment culminated and from now on receded more and more into the background. He interpreted the negative results of his attempt as "a hint from Providence."[40]

For a few years Kierkegaard retained the thought of seeking an appointment to the pastoral training college. This thought was of later origin and probably was responsible for his preparing a series of lectures on "The Dialectic of Ethical and Ethical-Religious Communication," of which we have not only extensive drafts but two finished lectures.[41] As far as we can see, it was Kierkegaard himself who in 1849 broached to Mynster the idea of an appointment to the pastoral training college. "The other day I went to Mynster and dropped a few hints about an appointment to the pastoral training college." But directly afterward came Kierkegaard's customary misgivings: "If they offered it to me, it would almost tempt me."[42] From subsequent conversations about this with Mynster we gather that Mynster did not look with favor on it, probably would have preferred to have Kierkegaard out in the country as a pastor.[43]

Kierkegaard held on to the thought of an appointment to the pastoral training college for a long time, perhaps because Mynster was unsympathetic. Even in August 1851 he raised the question with Mynster, as we learn in the following entry: "So I let fall a

few words about the pastoral training college just like that."[44]
As late as 1852 Kierkegaard deplored that Mynster had not offered
him a position at the pastoral training college.[45]

During all this concern over his financial situation, which for a
time he believed would be remedied by seeking an appointment,
Kierkegaard tried to struggle ahead to the trust that providence
would guide him. In this connection he reached the understanding
that "renunciation is a higher relationship to God," and wrote
enthusiastically about it. "The way renunciation is usually represented, it has appeared to me to be an attempt to make God into
a ridiculous pedant and the God-relationship into a perpetual
stinginess and incessant pettiness. Therefore it has not appealed
to me. But it is not that way at all, for renunciation, yes, the delight
of renunciation, is simply love's understanding with God. As far as
I am concerned, I owe it to truth to admit that it was God who
intimated it. I had not dreamed of it, nor had I believed myself
capable of it. But it was as if God whispered to me the secret: Renunciation is a higher relationship to God, is really the relationship of love. And thereupon I began, to say the least, to be fas-
cinated with renunciation—I have never before been so fasci-
nated."[46]

But it was still not so easy to get the better of his economic concerns, and even in 1854 Kierkegaard wrote the following: "That
which takes the most out of me in the long run is the thought of
what is going to happen, and it is coming closer and closer."[47]

We draw near to the last phase in the struggle between the poet
and the pastor. The main feature of this phase was that Kierkegaard as author attempted at a crucial point to actualize the high
ideal of a pastor which he finally formed.

But first a brief account of the separate stages during the time
immediately preceding this phase. It was in this period that Kier-
kegaard published the two most vigorously polemical books: *The
Sickness unto Death* (1849) and *Training in Christianity* (1850).
In these two works, especially in *Training in Christianity*, the
Christian demands are raised up so high that Kierkegaard did not

think himself able to fulfill them and therefore published them pseudonymously (Anti-Climacus).

With his challenge to the contemporary age through these two books Kierkegaard actually brought his authorship to a close.[48] From September 1851 until December 1854 he published nothing. But he worked unremittingly with various questions of central Christian significance. Kierkegaard himself valued the worth of these thoughts and reflective struggle very highly. In March 1853 he wrote: "A deep melancholy was repressed by writing. Thus the years passed by. Then worry over the future pressured me more and more. And it occurred to me that this enormous productivity was almost a grandiose diversion.

"Well, now it has stopped. It was difficult to do. For a few years now I have not been productive; consequently it is halted.

"The result has been that now once again there is collected, so to speak, in my mind and in my thoughts an enormous productivity —yes, at this moment I believe that a copious supply of various professors and poets could be made out of me."[49]

Kierkegaard did not use his wealth of thoughts for the publication of new works. But through his abundant journal entries for these years we are able to trace closely the subjects which were central to his interests. Only a few will be named here.

Kierkegaard was very much interested in the relation between the Church and the state; through a prolonged concentration upon the early years of Christianity he tried to come to a closer definition of "the militant Church" (*Training in Christianity*) in contrast to the distortions of Christianity which according to Kierkegaard had taken place in subsequent years. In connection with this he investigated such categories as the voluntary, witness to the truth, and imitation of Christ.

But many of his reflections still concerned his own position as author. When he looked back on his life it was clear to him that to him had been granted, as he says, the extraordinary.[50] He was still not sure what would be required of him in the future. He rejected for various reasons the thought of becoming a martyr in the cause of Christianity. Kierkegaard then attempted to become completely clear about his limitations and his position as the extraordinary, and he touched upon this subject in many journal entries.

Of the many different ideas he grappled with in the journals there is only one which he believed would lead him out again into action in the external world, as in the period of *The Corsair*, but this time with an essentially more serious perspective. He had gradually collected a whole arsenal of weapons with which he could attack existing Christendom, and he now began to perceive that this was the point where he was to take action, since he must declare judgment upon Christendom.

This thought came to him as early as 1852, when he wrote the following: "There is a word which should be said and which I should say; but it will bring with it such enormous consequences that it is as if I had no power to say it in this life."[51]

The following year he expressed this thought even more clearly: "There is something very definite I have to say, and it lies on my conscience in such a way that I feel as if I dare not die without having said it."[52] Only an occasion was required for the attack on the Church to begin and for Kierkegaard to speak with a heavy heart "the very definite word he had to say."

With this we have reached his last position in the struggle between the poet and the pastor. This position is delineated in the writings attacking the Church. Through these Kierkegaard attempted to realize in part the kind of public communication which to him seemed to be the highest ideal of Christian preaching, namely, directly addressing men on the streets and byways.

In this manner, then, Kierkegaard, who as religious author had previously merely operated with ideal possibilities, now entered into the world of actuality and attempted to actualize a synthesis of the religious poet and the ideal of a pastor.

Thoughts about the kind of communication which Kierkegaard practiced in the Church struggle are to be found back in his preparation (1847) of "The Dialectic of Ethical and Ethical-Religious

Communication." There Kierkegaard points out that a consistent ethical communication always uses the medium of actuality. The teacher must, as the saying goes, "live and teach on the street." In this connection Kierkegaard quotes Luther's remark that preaching should be done on the streets. "Luther says quite correctly that preaching should really be done on the streets rather than in churches."[53]

The next time Kierkegaard expressed the thought was in 1848 in relation to Mynster. "For Mynster it was just as impossible, yes, the most impossible of all, to preach in the square. And yet this preaching in churches has almost become paganism and theatricality, and Luther is quite right in urging that there really should be no preaching in the churches."[54]

After that the thought about preaching on the streets became more prominent for Kierkegaard. In 1851 he wrote, among other things: "To preach from the pulpit is to accuse oneself; if it is to be done, one ought to have the courage to apply it to himself.

"Then there is some truth in this kind of preaching, but nevertheless, in a stricter sense, real preaching or proclamation is preaching on the street and by acting."[55]

At the time of the attack on the Church, Kierkegaard upbraided Luther in a journal entry entitled "Why I have used this paper" *(Fædrelandet—The Fatherland)*, because Luther certainly had said that we should preach on the streets but he did not practice this himself. "Somewhere in one of his sermons Luther says that there really should not be preaching in the churches; he says this in a sermon admittedly held in a church; consequently in saying it he did not do so in earnest."[56]

Continuing on the same question Kierkegaard wrote: "Consequently there should not be preaching in the church but on the street, in the middle of life, in the actuality of the daily, week-day life." Kierkegaard explained further that his use of the paper *The Fatherland* for the attack on the Church was an approach toward preaching on the street or bringing essential Christianity, the thought of the essential Christianity, "right into the middle of life's actuality and into conflict with its variations. . . ." We can add here that the approach is even more true of his pamphlets *Øieblikket* (*The Moment,* 1854-55). Through these pamphlets Kierkegaard could address himself directly to the man on the street, to the common man, whom he esteemed.[57]

With this kind of communication Kierkegaard was able to stir up his age without himself becoming victimized. But he was very much occupied with the thought of going so far that the age might possibly prepare a fate for him similar to that which his two great prototypes received: Socrates, his human prototype, and Christ, his divine prototype.

In a journal entry with the heading "To influence catastrophically" he wrote concerning these reflections: "How anxious men would become for me if they came to know this, how strange this would seem to them: certainly that which has occupied me recently is whether or not God wants me to set everything in motion to bring about a catastrophe, get arrested, condemned, and possibly executed."[58]

With this final attempt to bring a religious poet's world of thought as near as possible to the world of actuality and existence, the struggle between poet and pastor reached its climax. The tension between the two was never entirely eased, but it became channeled through Kierkegaard's steadily deeper dependence on God, as is evident in the following passage in this same entry:

"And there is in my soul a concern that if I refrain from doing this I shall eternally repent of it, an apprehension which cannot be opposed, as far as I know, except by the thought in which I constantly commit myself to God—that he will keep watch so that I neglect nothing which I would have to repent of eternally because of its omission."

Howard V. Hong and Edna H. Hong

AN INTRODUCTION
TO *ARMED NEUTRALITY* AND
AN OPEN LETTER
Their Situation and Significance

Armed Neutrality[1] and *An Open Letter*[2] belong together with Kierkegaard's *On My Work as an Author* and *The Point of View for My Work as an Author;* all four were written around 1848-51. All are rooted in Kierkegaard's wrestling with the question of indirect communication and the poetic approach on the one hand and direct written communication, "stepping forth in character," and "action in the situation of actuality" on the other. Although the published works during this period are more than enough for even a more than ordinary lifetime, for Kierkegaard the period was primarily one of reflection on the termination of his poet-existence and publishing, and on the possibilities of direct action in the form of seeking an ordinary appointment as a pastor, of explicit declaration of his aims, and of direct critique on the age.

If the period 1848-51 was pivotal in terms of a shift from indirect communication to direct (and this includes *The Sickness unto Death* and *Training in Christianity*, even though under a pseudonym, Anti-Climacus; see X[1] A 510, p. 88 below), it was also the germination period for the direct critique culminating in the articles in *The Fatherland* and the pamphlets under the common title *The Moment* in the very last months of Kierkegaard's life in 1854-55. Therefore *Armed Neutrality* and *An Open Letter* are related directly also to events and writings of Kierkegaard's last years.

Kierkegaard undertook the publication of *An Open Letter*, and repeatedly contemplated the publication of *Armed Neutrality*, as needed steps in direct communication. Readers and interpreters of Kierkegaard at the present time are also in need of them, as is indicated even now, for example, by the much too conjectural and suppositional introduction to a new edition (1966) of *The Book on Adler (On Authority and Revelation)*. Dr. Gregor Malantschuk, one of the most discerning students of Kierkegaard in Europe today, in his background essay "Søren Kierkegaard—Poet or Pastor?" at the beginning of this volume, has provided an additional aid to our comprehension of this crucial period in the thought and life of a crucial thinker of the nineteenth and twentieth centuries.

Of the works mentioned, only the brief *On My Work as an Author* and *An Open Letter* were published during Kierkegaard's lifetime. *The Point of View* was published posthumously. *Armed Neutrality* remained in the unpublished papers even though Kierkegaard several times considered its publication in various ways; it was published as part of the *Papirer*,[3] but only in 1965 did it appear in Danish as a separate volume belonging to the *Works*, as E. Hirsch justifiably urged over thirty years ago. Inasmuch as *Armed Neutrality* and *An Open Letter* have a copious context in the burgeoning journals and papers of the period, a selection of the entries in the *Papirer* has been included in this volume together with the first English translations of *Armed Neutrality* and *An Open Letter*.

From the beginning Kierkegaard's published writings had a double track of indirect and direct communication, with the pseudonymous "esthetic" works on one side and on the other the "upbuilding or edifying" works under his own name. Usually a publication on one side was accompanied within a short time by publication on the other (see IX A 228, p. 72 below). Kierkegaard's intention to terminate the indirect, pseudonymous series is embodied in the very first word of the title *Concluding Unscientific Postscript to the Philosophical Fragments* (1846), and the work closes with a signed statement about the pseudonymous works. In the next two and one-half years he published four works under his own name: *A Literary Review* [*En literair Anmeldelse*], 1846; *Edifying Discourses in Various Spirits* [*Opbyggelige Taler i forskjellig Aand*], 1847; *Works of Love*, 1847; and *Christian Discourses*, 1848. Despite his plan, he could not resist the pseudonymous parallel, and in 1848 there appeared a pseudonymous work, *The Crisis and a Crisis in the Life of an Actress*. This, then, together with the second edition of the early pseudonymous work *Either/Or*, was to be the final end of indirect and pseudonymous communication, the work of the poet-philosopher in the interest of finding a man "where he is."[4]

For Kierkegaard in the period 1848-51 the question of more direct communication had two aspects. One of these pertained to the direct declaration of his aims and mode of working. *Armed Neutrality, An Open Letter, The Point of View for My Work as an Author*, and *On My Work as an Author*, as well as his uncharacteristically open friendship with Professor Rasmus Nielsen, were tokens of Kierkegaard's growing sense that in the long run there is something demonic in a continuous maieutic method, at least where Christianity and human instruments are involved (IX A 260, p. 72 below). At the same time he was unable to break his reserve, just as he had been unable in 1846 to halt the practice of using pseudonyms. In part this inability was simply reluctance to intrude his own person into a direct presentation, because an author's personality and life tend to become merely "interesting" material for the public and a distraction from the works for a reader. Therefore only the much-condensed *On My Work as an Author*, which included brief parts from *Armed Neutrality*, was published—and even this not until two years after it was written. Another kind of direct communication appeared in the form of "Has a Man the Right to Let Himself Be Put to Death for the Truth?" and "Of the Difference Between a Genius and an Apostle" (*Two Minor Ethical-Religious Treatises*, by H. H., 1849),[5] *The Sickness unto Death* (1849), and *Training in Christianity* (1850). The latter two works were under a pseudonym, Anti-Climacus, not by way of in-

direction, but because the ideality of the presentation transcended
Kierkegaard's own actuality. In substance and form they are direct
presentations of a Christian anthropology and the Christian life.
In 1851 a third direct communication, *For Self-Examination*, appeared under Kierkegaard's name.

The other aspect of direct communication involved "stepping
forth in character," "action in the situation of actuality." It would
be consonant with the termination of the work of the poet-philosopher to diminish the poetic-reflective distance through expression
in action, possibly eventuating in personal collision, through witnessing directly at risk to oneself. The entry of April 18, 1848 (VIII[1]
A 640, p. 58 below) is clear: "My whole nature is changed. . . . I am
free to speak." But only through agonizing reflection did he gradually approach more closely this glimpse of release from "closed-
upness" or reserve [*Indesluttethed*] and from the burden of his
melancholy and his penitential past. The entries on forgiveness
and imitation are especially prominent during this period, and they
mark the progress of the inner release which Kierkegaard came to
know more and more and also the way in which the requirement
impinged upon him. This method of direct engagement began
with issuing *Training in Christianity* and more particularly and
polemically with *An Open Letter*, a double attack on politically-
minded ecclesiastical reformers and secularized Christendom. In
these works the additional point was made that direct collision with
the established order might be required in Christian witness,
though not for the purpose of changing political-ecclesiastical externals and machinery.

ARMED NEUTRALITY

In 1838 Kierkegaard first employed the expression "armed neutrality" in an entry of a single line (II A 770, p. 57, below) . At that
time he probably had the Danish literary scene in mind. He had
just published his first work, *From the Papers of One Still Living*

(*S.V.* XIII, pp. 41-92), a criticism of Hans Christian Andersen "as a romantic poet, with constant reference to his latest work, *Only a Fiddler.*" But the small work also contains some of Kierkegaard's views on art, such as a poet's relation to his productions. Therefore the first time he used the expression "armed neutrality" he presumably wanted to indicate that he had certain definite views on esthetics which he was prepared to defend if necessary (see II A 768-85).

By 1848, when he used the expression again, it had taken on a deeper and more inclusive meaning. In the intervening decade he had written and published important works intended to delineate the existential possibilities of human life and to portray essential Christianity as distinguished from the domesticated, modified version of Christendom. In order to emphasize his views more clearly and directly, he considered publishing a periodical. "Presumably it would be the right thing at some time to give my contemporaries a definite and non-reduplicated idea of what I myself mean, what I am aiming at, etc. This is what I have in mind as the program of *Armed Neutrality,* a periodical, which would come out simultaneously with the second edition of *Either/Or.* In it I would scrutinize Christianity piece by piece and get the coil spring set in place" (IX A 212).

While preparing *Armed Neutrality* Kierkegaard abandoned the idea of giving an account of his position in a periodical. He called the work a book, and considered publishing it together with various other works in various combinations. (See the Chronological Table and the pertinent entries, mentioned there, from the journals and papers in the present volume.) In any case he did not want to publish it as an independent work. Finally from among the various works he published *The Sickness unto Death, Training in Christianity,* and *On My Work as an Author.* The last comprises the brief work "The Accounting" (which includes some expressions and ideas from *Armed Neutrality*) and a supplementary statement, "My Position as a Religious Writer in 'Christendom' and My Tactics."

It is fortunate that the manuscript of *Armed Neutrality* has been preserved in the *Papirer*, because, as Dr. Malantschuk states in the first Danish edition of *Armed Neutrality* as a separate volume (1965): "Even though *Armed Neutrality* is only a small work, it can give us particularly important information on those essential points in a new view of Christianity which Kierkegaard wanted his contemporaries to see. In no other work has Kierkegaard expressed himself so openly and with such wide perspectives on these matters as he has in *Armed Neutrality*."[6]

AN OPEN LETTER
TO DR. RUDELBACH

Andreas Gottlob Rudelbach (1792-1862) was the Danish son of Saxon J. H. Gottlob Rudelbach and Swedish Birgitte Østrom. In 1817 he won a university gold medal for a study of "The Nature and Value of Dithyrambic Poetry" and in 1822 was granted a doctor's degree by the University of Copenhagen for his thesis on the principles of ethics. The following year he travelled in Germany, Switzerland, and France. In 1825, together with N. F. S. Grundtvig, he began the publication of *Theologisk Maanedsskrift (Theological Monthly);* he continued it from Volume VI through Volume XIII (1828) alone because Grundtvig had been censured officially. The journal usually contained a polemic against the reigning rationalism. He impressed students, H. L. Martensen in particular, by a "combination of earnestness and keenness but especially by his prodigious learning and his large library."[7] With little chance of getting an appointment in Denmark because of his Grundtvigianism and his opposition to dogmatic rationalism, Rudelbach accepted an appointment in Saxony as head pastor and councillor in Blauchau. After an active, influential, and scholarly career in Germany he returned to Denmark in 1845. He broke with Grundtvig because of disagreement on apostolic symbols as "the living word." H. N. Clausen and others were opposed to his appointment to the university divinity faculty, and after lecturing 1847-1848 as *privat-docent* Rudelbach gave up thought of an academic appointment and was named pastor of St. Mikkels, Slagelse, Sjælland, Denmark. A series of writings in Danish (essentially Grundtvigian and free-church in outlook) included, in 1846, *Christelig Biographie (Christian Biography)*, which Kierkegaard read and appreciated, and in 1851, *Om det borgerlige Ægteskab (On Civil Marriage)*, the occasion of Kierkegaard's *An Open Letter*.

Three times in his life Kierkegaard ventured into uncharacteristic direct controversy: with Meir Goldschmidt and *The Corsair* on the issue of depraved anonymous journalism, with A. G. Rudelbach on the issue of politicizing reformation of the Church, and later with H. L. Martensen and the established order on the main issue of the acculturized, emasculated Christianity of Christendom. In each case the primary concern was an issue, not a person. Goldschmidt and Kierkegaard each had a certain respect for the other. Rudelbach and Kierkegaard were acquainted through visits and conversations in the remarkable home of M. P. Kierkegaard. Martensen had been Kierkegaard's teacher and was a scholar and professor of eminence. Furthermore, in all three instances Kierkegaard initiated the battle because of the important issues at stake.

The three engagements became intertwined in *An Open Letter*. One strand was the politicizing and sectarianizing of Church reformation by Rudelbach. This involved Bishop Mynster (whom Martensen, an early admirer of Rudelbach, succeeded and called "a witness.")[8] It also drew in Goldschmidt and the aftermath of the unresolved *Corsair* controversy because of Mynster's bland obliviousness to what was at stake in the *Corsair* controversy and in Kierkegaard's critique of Rudelbach. To Kierkegaard this was a token of Mynster's obtuseness in trying to accommodate Christianity to the mediocre mentality of the age. Although he was deeply attached to Mynster personally, Kierkegaard reluctantly initiated an attack on the Bishop's apostasy of accommodation after Martensen's "witness" eulogy. Although *An Open Letter* (January 31, 1851) was in one sense a defense of Mynster against sectarian, politicizing reformers, it was, together with *Training in Christianity* (September 11, 1850) and *For Self-Examination* (September 10, 1851) the beginning of a direct critique of the establishment because of its "modifications" and devitalization of Christianity. Therefore *An Open Letter* is important both as a direct declaration of Kierkegaard's position and as a signal bell of what was to come.

Although the two pieces, *Armed Neutrality* and *An Open Letter*, are short, they provide a compact and explicit presentation of Kierkegaard's own interpretation of his life and work. Furthermore, they epitomize his own struggle over the indirect and direct methods. In a sense they are a pair of personal punctuation marks, the colon and the dash—personal because they were his favorite punctuation marks and personal also because he was at a penultimate point in the climactic sentence of his life. Within eight months after *An Open Letter* only three small publications appeared, all under his own name, and for three years thereafter there was an unusual silence. Then came the terminating series of direct action communications culminating in the issues of *The Moment*.

Apart from the interpretive value for a present-day reader and student of Kierkegaard, the two pieces are of significance also for the pungent posing of issues even more crucial now than one hundred years ago. Of most importance here and central also now are the twin tendencies of an emptying accommodation in religion and the Church on the one hand and an instrumentalizing, exploitationary approach to religion and the Church in the interests of political power, artistic patronage, social utility, etc. on the other. But the two are complementary and are easily merged. Kierkegaard's counsel is still cogent: first of all for awareness of how it is with us and with each one and a forthright admission of our situation. This is the Kierkegaard of religious intransigence and cultural relevance, of individual reformatory initiative and social implication.

Søren Kierkegaard

ARMED NEUTRALITY

or

My Position as a Christian Author
in Christendom

By this phrase "armed neutrality,"[1] especially as I get it defined more and more precisely, I believe I am able to characterize the position I intend to take and have taken in illuminating Christianity, or what Christianity is, or, more accurately, what is involved in being a Christian. Naturally, it cannot mean that I want to leave undecided the question of whether or not I myself am a Christian, am pursuing it, fighting for it, praying about it, and hoping before God that I am that. What I have wanted to *prevent* and want to *prevent* now is any sort of impression that I am a Christian to any extraordinary degree, a remarkable kind of Christian. This I have wished to prevent and still wish to prevent. What I have wanted to *achieve* and still want to *achieve* through my work, what I still regard to be of utmost importance, is first of all to get clarified what is involved in being a Christian, to present a picture of a Christian in all its ideality—that is, the true form and stature worked out to the very last detail, submitting myself before all others to judgment by this picture, whatever the judgment is, or, more accurately, precisely this judgment—that I do not resemble the picture. In addition, because the task of producing this ideal picture is a work in which emphasis falls upon differentiating the qualifications for doing this work,[2] especially since it is to be carried out in the context of the manifold confusions abroad in modern times,[3] I have chosen for purposes of designation the words: *neutrality* and *armed*.

I believe it is an overstatement to say that Christianity in our time has been completely abolished. No, Christianity is still present and in its truth, but as a *teaching*, as *doctrine*. What has been abolished and forgotten, however (and this can be said without exaggeration), is *existing as a Christian*, what it means to be Christian; what has been lost, what is no longer present, so to speak, is the ideal picture of what it is to be a Christian.

That this is the state of affairs can be perceived readily in the nature of the confusion. (1) Christendom is something established. This is confusing, because it is really impossible to be a Christian in this way, since an establishment as the true arena for religiousness gives all Christian qualifications an unchristian, conciliatory perspective upon the temporal; whereas the true Christian perspective for every Christian qualification is polemically oriented toward finitude or out of it toward the eternal. Relaxed piety is Jewish piety;[4] Christianity or being a Christian is a battling piety (engaged at two points, first with oneself in order to become a Christian and then with the world's opposition and persecution because one is Christian). (2) Every decisive qualification of being Christian is according to a dialectic or is on the other side of a dialectic. The confusion is that, with the help of the scientific-scholarly abrogation of the dialectical element, this has been completely forgotten. In this way, instead of, as we suppose, going further than original Christianity, we have thrown Christianity back into the esthetic. Actually to be, to exist (the single individual), consists of the dialectical element; what speculation calls unity is first achieved in eternity and only momentarily in time. By cavalierly permitting the dialectical element in existence, the existence of the single individual, to be abrogated in this way, we have abolished, if I may use the expression, all the navigation marks with regard to being a Christian. It is possible that current Christendom is the most perfect form of Christianity that has ever been seen; it is also possible that it is thoroughgoing secularism.[5] (3) The medium for being Christian has been shifted from existence and the ethical to the intellectual, the metaphysical, the imaginary; a more or less theatrical relationship has been introduced between thinking Christianity and being Christian—and thus being a Christian has been abolished.

Therefore what has to be brought into prominence again above all is the ideal picture of a Christian, so that it can appear as a task, beckoning, and on the other hand, so that it can crush with all its weight the presumptuousness[6] of wanting to go beyond being Christian, something which can be explained only by the fact that what it means to be Christian has been forgotten.

It is this ideal picture that I have tried to present and shall keep on trying to present. The reader will kindly be patient and not rush at once to judge or estimate to what extent the particular individual also serves to illuminate this picture. From the very beginning my work has not been a labor of haste, has not been an impetuous amendment[7] to the wholesale confusion or a new patch on an old garment.[8] Be patient—and perhaps I do have a kind of right to ask this, since even more patience is required to carry through the project—be patient, then, and attentive.

Therefore my task is and has been to present in every way the ideal picture of being a Christian: dialectically, pathetically (in the various forms of pathos),[9] and in terms of an understanding of man, modernized by constant reference to modern Christendom and to the errors of a scientific-scholarly outlook. Jesus Christ himself, of course, is the prototype [*Forbilledet*] and will continue to be that, unchanged until the end. But Christ is also much more than the prototype; he is the object of faith. In Scripture he is presented chiefly as such, and this is why he is presented more in being than in becoming, or really only in being, and therefore all the middle terms[10] are lacking—which everyone is aware of who humbly and prayerfully has earnestly sought to order his life according to his example. Furthermore, in the course of time, unchanged Christianity nevertheless has been subject to modifications in relation to the changing world. I certainly do not hold that it is Christianity which is supposed to be improved and perfected by new modifications—I am not that speculative. No, my thought is that unchanged Christianity at times may need to secure itself by way of new modifications against the new, the new nonsense in the world. Let me clarify this by reference to something else. In the far, far distant past, times more simple than these, it was the custom to draw up legal documents such as contracts. But if we take such a contract from olden times and compare it with a contract of the same kind from 1848, we find the latter undeniably modified in important ways. But we should not draw the hasty conclusion that this one is better than the other one; ironically it might turn out that it would have been better, after all, if these modifications had not been necessary. But, since those simple times, there have been so many rascals and swindlers that modifications have become necessary. So also with the modifications which unchanged Christianity has undergone in the course of time—they are bad or because of evil but for the good. But in the process of modifying Christianity, what it is to be a Christian has also been modified. By the ideal picture of a Christian I understand in part a kind of human interpreting of Christ as the prototype, a human interpreting which, although he is and remains the object of faith, contains all the middle terms in relation to derivatives and casts everything into becoming—and in part the modifications related to the past confusions of a particular time.

But who, then, is to do this, who is to be the one who places this picture into the situation of actuality and holds it up? If someone comes rushing headlong, pointing to himself and saying, "I am the one, I myself am this ideal of a Christian"—then we have fanaticism and all its woeful consequences. God forbid that it should happen this way! As far as I am concerned, I do not believe that I could ever possibly do this. Nothing is more foreign to my being and to my natural qualifications (the dialectical) than fanaticism and fury. If I could be regarded as furious in any way, it might be said—and it probably is being said—that I have a furious discretion—that is, a discretion which could drive others into a fury. From the very beginning of my work as an author there no doubt has been a rather solitary person hidden here and there who has been aware of what I have been able to present poetically and has only been waiting for the moment when I should confuse myself with a poetic presentation and rush forth claiming myself to be the ideal, the awaited one, *etc.*—in order to attach himself to me as a disciple, a follower, and the like. He would therefore be driven into a rage by my discretion, which is maintained until finally he furiously wishes me dead or far away because I stand in his way, so that out of a kind of respect for me he is not able to pass himself off as being what he would have preferred me to be. In either way, therefore, I would be a hindrance to getting a fanatic movement going full blast.

It certainly is extremely important that the ideal picture of a Christian be held up in every generation, that it be illuminated particularly in relationship to the errors of the times, but the one who presents this picture must above all not make the mistake of identifying himself with it in order to pick up some followers, must not let himself be idolized and then with earthly and worldly passion pass judgment upon Christendom. No, the purely ideal relationship must be maintained. The one who presents this ideal must be the very first one to humble himself under it, and even though he himself is striving within himself to approach this ideal, he must confess that he is very far from being it. He must confess that he is related only poetically to this ideal picture or *qua* poet to the *presentation* of this picture, while he (and here he differs from the ordinary conception of a poet) personally and Christianly is related to the *presented* picture, and that only as a poet presenting the picture is he out in front.

In this way no fanaticism develops; the poet or, more accurately, the poet-dialectician, does not make himself out to be the ideal and even less does he judge any single human being. But he holds up the ideal so that everyone, if he has a mind to, in quiet solitariness can compare his own life with the ideal. To a certain extent the presentation of the ideal cannot possibly avoid being polemical, but it is not polemical against any particular person but is infinitely polemical only in order to illuminate the ideal; it has no proposal to make and does not lean toward some settlement in the external or the secular world.

This was and is my idea of a reformation, which, whether or not it succeeds and to whatever degree it succeeds or not, will go ahead on its own and take place without general assemblies, synods, voting—in short without profanation. During the few years I have been a writer I dare say I have been unusually prolific and productive, something which I feel has not diminished but has rather increased, but I have never had and do not have a single comma to offer to a general assembly or convention of secret balloters. I have had much to say and feel far from emptied; on the contrary, I feel that I still have much more to say, but I have never had and do not have a jot, not an infinitesimal iota, of anything which tempts secularly by being something new. There is only one thing which can halt a whirling around in every direction and thus also only one thing which can stop the whirling or the giddiness—and this is precisely the kind and degree of giddiness—in which the ideal little by little diminishes and is finally lost entirely—the giddiness that one is just as good a Christian as all the others and thus is a Christian simply by comparison; there is only one thing that can stop it—no general assembly, no balloting can do it, for they only foster the sickness—and this is that the single individual, instead of whirling around in constant comparison of himself to "the others," relates himself to the ideal.[11] In that very moment he is stopped forever—and even if he were to live a hundred years, he would never propose a general assembly.

In order to present this ideal with as much pathos, as truly and faithfully, and in polemics as correctly as I possibly can, I shall use every single day and ask for no wages—because for me this work is another expression of the fact that I myself am brought to a halt by the ideal—not as if I had grasped it, not as if I were it, for I am

so far from it that in a whole lifetime I very likely shall not finish
the task of properly discovering and rightly presenting the ideal.

Humble before God, knowing what I do of what it really means
truly to be a Christian, and knowing myself as I do, I dare not in
any way maintain that I am a Christian in any outstanding way or
permit any differentiating accent to fall on my being a Christian;
for example, I would not dare, particularly not in Christendom, to
expose myself to becoming a martyr, to being persecuted, to losing
my life because I am a Christian. Do not pass premature judgment
on what I am saying but rather take time to understand it. Too
many all too hastily protest that they are Christian to the degree
that they are willing to die for it; whereas the difficulty is possibly
at an entirely different point than they suspect. Let me take an
imaginary situation. With a sword hanging over my head I am ordered to declare whether or not I am a Christian. My answer would
be: I hope before God that I am a Christian, and I believe that out
of grace he will accept me as a Christian, and so on. If my captors
were not satisfied with the answer but said, "You must say either
that you are a Christian or that you are not," then I would answer:
No, this I will not do. If they persisted, "Then we will kill you because you will not answer as we demand," my answer would be: Go
ahead, I do not object; I understand and accept this martyrdom.
By this I mean I am not afraid of being killed—although I by no
means flaunt a willingness for it nor am I eager for it, and therefore I must ask the reader to remember that the discussion here is,
of course, hypothetical. What I do fear is what my death would
come to signify through what I say about myself. In other words,
I am not afraid of dying, but I am afraid of saying too much about
myself. I do not cravenly flee from a martyrdom, but I must understand myself and myself be convinced about the defensibility of
my falling as a martyr.

The question of whether I am a Christian (and for every single
individual, the question of whether he is a Christian) is entirely a

relationship to God. When I (and so it always is for the single individual) declare that I am Christian, I am really speaking with God, even though men have asked me and I therefore am speaking with men, and for this reason I dare not speak differently from the way I would speak with God. That is, as soon as I (and so it always is with the single individual) speak about my being a Christian, God hears it. I cannot speak of my being a Christian according to a merely human standard or within the sphere of human comparison. But, then, directly before God, do I dare say: I am a Christian? No, I do not dare do this—I least of all. But neither do I dare let the emphasis fall upon my being a Christian, that I am put to death because I am a Christian—for suppose God thinks otherwise and I have forgotten respectful deference to God, in my expression about myself have forgotten to express that God is the judge. If I were killed because I am a Christian (as a consequence of my own apodictic declaration),[12] my life would be taken—but this would be the least important part of it, I should by no means be through with it; for suppose I run into trouble in eternity, suppose that it was arrogance on my part apodictically, instead of hypothetically through reverence for God, to say that I am a Christian. I must indeed be judged, and on judgment day I consequently shall have to repeat that I was put to death because I, according to my own statement, was Christian. But if I say it, then I shall say in the presence of God that I was a Christian; it is true, nothing is more certain—since, after all, wasn't I killed because of being a Christian? But I would not dare say this to God under any circumstances. Face to face with God I would have to use a far humbler expression: I hope before God that in his mercy he will accept me as Christian.

Obviously it is not my intention or the intention of *Armed Neutrality* to abolish martyrs or to make martyrdom an impossibility. I merely move it reflectively into inwardness. (Meanwhile I do not let the martyr become so muddleheaded because he is about to be executed that he garbles what he says about his God-relationship, presumably because he is so occupied with his imminent martyrdom; instead let him be occupied solely with his God-relationship

and be like an absent-minded professor in respect to the martyrdom.) Generally the fact is overlooked that martyrdom is in the
category of freedom, that it is not "the others" who have the martyr
in their power but it is the martyr who has them in his power. They
can kill him, to be sure, but from a spiritual point of view he can
decide where he is going to fall. It is impossible to force a man to
declare something if it is against his will and he is willing therefore to give his life. Thus men may say: We are going to kill you
because you will not say it—to this he has no objection. There is a
power, a superior power rooted in willingness to make a sacrifice;
to the same degree to which a person is willing to sacrifice he has
this superior power. Therefore, where the martyrdom takes place
rests, so to speak, with the martyrs themselves. But to be the Christian openly before other men, to be killed because, by one's own
declaration, one is Christian—this can so very easily be a satisfaction
of human emotions.

Let us imagine the martyrdom I have suggested. One will not
say: I am Christian, but: I hope before God that I am Christian,
and the like. Thereupon he is told: Well, then, you will be killed
because you will not answer the way we want you to. To this he
replies: All right. So he is put to death. This is a martyrdom.
Through death he departs and enters eternity—for judgment. Under judgment he trusts that God in his mercy will accept him as
Christian—he has not said too much about himself. Indeed, the
more inwardness there is, the greater the fear and trembling before
God. Externally oriented thinking is preoccupied with having the
courage before men to become a martyr; inwardly oriented thinking is preoccupied with having the courage before God to be a
martyr. This is martyrdom's proper fear and trembling. Many a
pagan has also had the courage to be put to death for an idea, but
the pagan did not have the fear and trembling of the God-relationship.

Ideality with respect to being Christian means a continual inward deepening. The more ideal the conception of being a Christian, the more inward it becomes—and the more difficult. Being

Christian undergoes a change which can be clarified by a secular analogy. Formerly there were in Greece wise men called σοφοι. Then along came Pythagoras and with him the qualification of reflection, reduplication,[13] with respect to being a wise man; therefore he did not venture to call himself a wise man but instead called himself a φιλοσοφος (friend or lover of wisdom, philosopher). Was this a step backward or a step forward; or was it not that Pythagoras' ideals had encompassed what it really means to call oneself a wise man, what is really required for this; so that there was wisdom in his not even daring to call himself a wise man.[14]

Now to my *armed neutrality*. Indeed, it would not be impossible for me to experience martyrdom in one way or another, but truly, I want the basis of it precisely and definitely determined. I do not say that I am an outstanding Christian—I believe I should have failed in my task completely and should have misunderstood my individuality and all my qualifications entirely if I had exposed myself to any attack or persecution along these lines. But I do maintain that I know with uncommon clarity and definiteness what Christianity is, what can be required of the Christian, what it means to be Christian. To an unusual degree I have, I believe, the qualifications to portray this. I also believe it is my duty to do it, simply because it seems to be forgotten in Christendom, and obviously there is no probability that the present generation is capable of educating in Christianity. I think it is my duty to Christianity, my duty to what has been passed on from the fathers and was also entrusted to me by a father, whose upbringing is in large part the energizer of my activity. I am often reminded of the teachers of my childhood and youth, the admired and unforgettable principal of the Borgerdyds School, who wrote almost nothing about me in his report of me but wrote instead a eulogy on my father. I believe it is my clearly understood duty to do this, because a person so rigorously brought up in Christianity will soon be a great rarity.

But to do this undauntedly in the service of the truth can very well expose me to the opposition of men, insofar as they generally take a dim view of screwing up the price or the requirement for being what they already think they are, the title of which they do not want to give up. Here is the place where I do not intend to avoid any danger, even the most extreme, but rather, when a storm blows up in this direction, I understand my task to be precisely that of confronting the danger and remaining in it. Yet it must be clear that what I have fought for, and if I should fall, what I have fallen for, or if I come to suffer in one way or another, what I am suffering for—is not that I have claimed to have been the outstanding Christian but that in the service of the truth I have championed what it means to be a Christian.

Armed neutrality. If I were involved with pagans, I could not be neutral; then in opposition to them I should have to say that I am Christian. But I am living in Christendom among Christians or among men who all claim to be Christians. It is not up to me, a man, to judge others, particularly not in the role of one who knows men's hearts, which here would have to be the case. Now if I were to insist that I am Christian, what would this mean in the situation? It would mean that I am Christian in contrast to Christians—that is, that I am a Christian raised to the second power, the outstanding Christian. This is why I maintain neutrality in regard to my being Christian. On the other hand, this cannot possibly mean a denial of Christianity, for I am living in Christendom and am Christian just as are all the others. Moreover, I declare forthrightly that I am Christian in the sense that others are but not in contrast to them. This way I keep neutral, not in contrast to being Christian but in contrast to being a Christian raised to the second power. And so I work at portraying the Christian ideal. In order to do it, I must have this neutrality. How should I dare be so shameless as to occasion in the remotest manner the odious notion that I am talking about myself, or how should I in all modesty be capable of saying anything at all if I did not in every way avoid* the obscene, the odious notion that I am talking about myself.

* *In margin:* do the utmost, do everything to avoid

The task, then, is to portray the ideal Christian, and this is where I propose to do battle. If someone says to me, "What you say is untrue; you have a confused, false conception of what it is to be Christian"—then I shall answer: Enlighten me about it and I shall alter my conception; if not, then of course I shall not alter a jot. If whiners say to me, "Give up your enterprise, take back what you have done; spare us; this conception is terrifying for us, it screws up the price so much that we are brought to despair"—then I shall answer: No, not a jot. I, too, know the pain of it, but I neither dare nor can do otherwise. I pray God that in this respect he will Christianly harden my heart and mind to make me Christianly tough enough not to spoil it all with human pity. If they threaten me for the purpose of making me abandon my enterprise out of the fear of men, or making my hand shake and bungle the picture, I pray God that whatever danger comes in the form of bloody persecution or in the form of mockery, laughter, and ridicule, whether the suffering is physical or psychical, he will give me strength not to deviate a hair's breadth from what I understand to be the truth.

This is my idea of the judgment which I believe is going to fall upon Christendom: not that I or any single individual shall judge others, but the ideal picture of what it is to be a Christian will judge me and everyone who permits himself to be judged. In a finite sense the ideal picture accosts no one; it has the infinite distance of the ideal from all hasty earthly judgment and prejudgment of this one and that one or of these particular actual persons; when the ideal is used in this way it has already been debased.

It is completely accidental that I am the one who has the task of portraying this picture. But someone has to do it. Honor, esteem, or other earthly advantage certainly will not come my way because of it. To make it a sound piece of work, the wages will be analogous to the honorarium the true Christian gets in the world, but only in a somewhat mitigated form, not in the form of suffering because I am Christian but only (in the mitigated form of suffering) in my capacity as poet, philosopher, etc. The mitigated form is, of course, proof of my imperfection, proof that I am not the true Christian. Away with that childish talk which uses the winning of earthly advantage as proof that I am willing the true and the good. No, it is always the opposite which proves, Christianly, that one or whether one really wills the good and the true. That I nevertheless do enjoy some esteem in the world proves, I regret, only how imperfect I still am; and the fact that I probably shall get through life somehow, tested only in a mitigated sort of martyrdom, proves, of course, that I have not pursued it to perfection.

Finally, if some impetuous pate, who knows at once whether or not he is Christian, finds it remarkable that the person who was capable of presenting this picture and uninterruptedly occupied himself with thoughts like this did not himself know definitely whether he is Christian, I should answer thus: I did not say that, but I did say that to say to oneself that he is Christian means to speak with God, and that therefore a human being must speak with fear and trembling. Having said this, for the sake of that impetuous pate (who in speaking of himself perhaps regards himself as one of those more profound characters who feel a deep need for positiveness, somewhat like those who in respect to love regard themselves as more profound characters who are not satisfied with love but feel a deep need—for external certainty) I shall add, *in usum Delphini*,[15] an example of a remarkable sort of slowness in a somewhat similar direction. Men with impetuous pates naturally know at once and very definitely that they are human beings. Now I dare say I am right in maintaining that not many have lived who knew human nature as well as did Socrates, who knew himself, besides. And the *summa summarum* of his knowledge in his seventieth year was that he did not definitely know whether or not he was a human being.[16] How can this be explained? I wonder if this was not because he had employed his time primarily in thinking about what it means to be human? This is done very quickly by impetuous pates because they leap over the question, assume that they know —and then in all precipitateness there appears that remarkable being (who could give a slower person much to think about and make, it would seem, even the impetuous one himself a little slower): a human being who knows definitely that he is a human being but does not know definitely what it means to be human. Surely there have been thousands of Christians of the same sort: they know definitely that they are Christians but do not know definitely what it means to be Christian. Nevertheless, it is still possible, perhaps, by continuous diligence over a number of years to pursue this to the point of *knowing* definitely what it means to be Christian; whether one himself is that cannot be *known*, surely not with definiteness—it must be believed, and in faith there is always fear and trembling.

Søren Kierkegaard

AN OPEN LETTER

Prompted by a Reference to Me by
Dr. Rudelbach[1]

The reference is on page 70 [of Dr. Rudelbach's *Om det borger-lige Ægteskab (On Civil Marriage)*].

The text reads: "Surely the deepest and highest interest of the Church in our day is . . . . . to become emancipated particularly from what is rightly called *habitual* and *legally established Christianity.*"

The footnote reads: "'This is the same point that one of our outstanding contemporary writers, *Søren Kierkegaard*, has sought to inculcate, to impress, and, as *Luther* says, to drive home to all who will listen."

Then the text continues immediately with the following sentence: "But for this emancipation civil marriage is an important, perhaps indispensable, instrument, a necessary link in the marshalling of all the measures which signify and condition the ushering in of religious freedom."

Consequently, all those numerous, qualitatively different pseudonymous works all the way from *Either/Or,* and in addition all my variegated edifying or upbuilding works, all these are packed together under one heading and called: Søren Kierkegaard.[2]

But now to the statement itself. The idiom "It is just a half-truth" fits it fairly accurately—that is, the first half, taken literally, is true and the second half is false.*

---

* Yet even in the first half (about "habitual Christianity") the expression "emancipate" must not be stressed, lest it be thought that in my activity I

I am a hater of "habitual Christianity." This is true. I hate habitual Christianity in whatever form it appears. I would like particular notice to be made of this "in whatever form," for habitual Christianity can indeed have many forms. And if there were no other choice, if the choice were only between the sort of habitual Christianity which is a secular-minded thoughtlessness that nonchalantly goes on living in the illusion of being Christian, perhaps without ever having any impression of Christianity, and the kind of habitual Christianity which is found in the sects, the enthusiasts, the super-orthodox, the schismatics[3]—if worst came to worst, I would choose the first. The first kind has still taken Christianity in vain only in a thoughtless and negative way, if on the whole it may be judged even that rigorously. The second kind has taken Christianity in vain perhaps out of spiritual pride, but in any case in a positive way. One could almost be tempted to smile at the first kind, because there is hope; the second makes one shudder. But, as stated, it is true that I am a hater of habitual Christianity. Therefore I can have no objection if our learned theologian, Dr. Rudelbach, says something like this; on the contrary, I would even thank him for it, all the more since I became acquainted with this man in my father's house and am convinced that he is genuinely well-disposed toward me. Nor do I object if in the future Dr. R. privately includes me in his prayers, that I may unto the end maintain this hatred of all habitual Christianity, which I trust and hope Dr. R. also will keep, even though I perhaps am aware of forms of habitual Christianity which have come less to his attention. The only thing I wish in this matter is that in the future he would not associate that misleading term "emancipation" with my efforts, and the only thing I might fear is that, after I have said this myself, it will become a literary cliché to write that I am a hater of all habitual Christianity.

---

meant to employ external means or proposed their use, nor must the word "Church" be stressed, lest it be forgotten that I have been concerned only with "the single individual" [*den Enkelte*]; otherwise this half also becomes untrue. This is why I say the idiom "It is just a half-truth" fits "fairly accurately," for taken strictly it is not even half true.

Now to the second half of the statement. I am supposed to have taken a position against "legally established Christianity" or "state-Christianity." Yes, this Søren Kierkegaard's whole intention is supposed to be to attack established Christianity—more specifically, to fight for the emancipation of the Church from the state, or at least "to inculcate, to impress, to drive this home."

In Ursin's *Arithmetic*,[4] which was used in my school days, a reward was offered to anyone who could find a miscalculation in the book. I also promise a reward to anyone who can point out in these numerous books a single proposal for external change, or the slightest suggestion of such a proposal, or even anything which in the remotest way even for the most nearsighted person at the greatest distance could resemble an intimation of such a proposal or of a belief that the problem is lodged in externalities, that external change is what is needed, that external change is what will help us.

In proportion to the capacities granted to me and also with various self-sacrifices I have diligently and honestly worked for the inward deepening of Christianity in myself and in others insofar as they are willing to be influenced. But simply because from the beginning I have understood Christianity to be inwardness and my task to be the inward deepening of Christianity, I have overscrupulously seen to it that not a passage, not a sentence, not a line, not a word, not a letter has slipped in about a proposal for external change or suggesting a belief that the problem is lodged in externalities, that external change is what is needed, that external change is what will help us.

There is nothing about which I have greater misgivings than all that even slightly tastes of this disastrous confusion of politics and Christianity, a confusion which can very easily bring about a new kind and mode of Church-reformation, a reverse reformation which in the name of reformation puts something new and worse in place of something old and better, although it is still supposed to be an honest-to-goodness reformation, which is then celebrated by floodlighting the entire city.

Christianity is inwardness, inward deepening. If at a given time the forms under which one has to live are not the most perfect, if they can be improved, in God's name do so. But *essentially* Christianity is inwardness. Just as man's advantage over animals is to be able to live in any climate, so also Christianity's perfection, simply because it is inwardness, is to be able to live, according to its vigor, under the most imperfect conditions and forms, if such be the case. Politics is the external system, this Tantalus-like[5] activity aimed at external change.

It is apparent from his latest work that Dr. R. believes that Christianity and the Church are to be saved by "the free institutions." If this faith in the saving power of politically achieved free institutions belongs to true Christianity, then I am no Christian, or even worse, I am a regular child of Satan, because, frankly, I am indeed suspicious of these politically achieved free institutions, especially of their saving, renewing power. Such is my Christianity, or so Christian-dumb am I, who, incidentally, have had nothing to do with "Church" and "state"—this is much too immense for me. Altogether different prophets are needed for this, or, quite simply, this task ought to be entrusted to those who are regularly appointed and trained for such things. I have not fought for the emancipation of "the Church" any more than I have fought for the emancipation of Greenland commerce, of women, of the Jews, or of anyone else. With my sights upon "the single individual," aiming at inward deepening in Christianity in "the single individual," with the weapons of the spirit, simply and solely with the weapons of the spirit, I have, as an individual, consistently fought to make the single individual aware of the "illusion" and to alert him against letting himself be deceived by it. Just as I regard it as an illusion for someone to imagine that it is external conditions and forms which hinder him in becoming a Christian, so is it also the same illusion if someone imagines that external conditions and forms will help him become a Christian.

I can understand a politician's counting on free institutions as an aid to the state, for politics is externality, which by its very nature has no life in itself but must borrow it from the forms, and thus there is this faith in forms. But that Christianity, which has life in itself, is supposed to be aided by the free institutions—this, according to my understanding, is a complete misconception of Christianity, which, where it is genuinely fervent inwardness, is infinitely higher and infinitely freer than all institutions, constitutions, etc. Christianity will not be helped from the outside by institutions and constitutions, and least of all if these are not won through suffering by martyrs in the old-fashioned Christian way but are won in a social and amicable political way, by elections or by a lottery of numbers. On the contrary, to be aided in this way is the downfall of Christianity. Christianity is victorious inwardness. This is what should be worked for, that this victorious inwardness may be in every man, if possible, that "the single individual" may become more and more truly a Christian. This is what should be done: self-concern must be awakened in "the single individual," the self-concern which infinitely gives him something other to think about than external forms, the self-concern which, when it has turned a person inward in this way, is transmuted under a higher influence into that victorious inwardness, although the self-concern still remains to protect him against becoming externalized again. Therefore, personally concerned, wounded by ideals and yet unspeakably joyful and grateful for this fact, I have fought for the ideals against "the illusions" in order to awaken this self-concern in "the single individual" by means of the vision of the ideals.

The difference between Dr. R. and me is quite obvious; this difference I must assert most definitely. There is also another obvious difference between us which I wish to stress. Dr. R. possesses amazing learning; as far as I know he is probably the most learned man in Denmark, and in my opinion we all ought to be happy to have such a learned man among us. On the other hand, in learning and scholarship, I am, especially by comparison, a poor bungler who knows enough arithmetic for household use. But I cannot remain silent about an appreciatory—and such an extravagantly appreciatory—asseveration of the significance of my activity as an author. I am really afraid that, brief though it is, it might manage "as Luther says, to drive home" this misunderstanding "to all those who will listen." And I have considered it my present duty to oppose—something which otherwise would hardly have occurred to me—and oppose somewhat more specifically than would otherwise have occurred to me—this misunderstanding, and also to keep any particular party, perhaps misled by Dr. R's words, from "the habit" of automatically enrolling me in the party.

S. Kierkegaard

Permit me to add the following, lest what I say be misunderstood, as if it were my view that Christianity consists purely and simply of putting up with everything in regard to external forms, without doing anything at all, as if Christianity did not know very well what is to be done—if worst comes to worst. But my entire activity as an author has had nothing to do with such an eventuality. I have only provided, poetically, what may be called an existential-corrective to the established order, oriented toward inward deepening in "the single individual"—that is, I am positive I have never directed one word against the teaching and the organization of the established order, but I have worked to make this teaching more and more the truth in "the single individual." And in order to prevent any misunderstanding I have aimed polemically throughout this whole undertaking at "the crowd," the numerical, also at the besetting sin of our time, self-appointed reformation and the falsifications along this line.

In Acts[6] we read: We ought to obey God rather than men. There are situations, therefore, in which an established order can be of such a nature that the Christian ought not put up with it, ought not say that Christianity means precisely this indifference to the external.

But now let us see how the apostles did not act, for everyone pretty well knows how those venerable ones did act.

The apostles did not go around talking among themselves saying: "It is intolerable that the Sanhedrin makes preaching the

Word punishable; it is a matter of conscience. What should we do about it? Should we not form a group and send an appeal to the Sanhedrin—or should we take it up at a synodical meeting? It is just possible that by combining with those who otherwise are our enemies we can manage a majority vote so that we can obtain freedom of conscience to proclaim the Word." Good Lord! Forgive me, venerable sirs, forgive me for having to speak this way. It was necessary.

On the contrary, how did they act?—for no doubt a good many have forgotten. Essentially "the apostle" is a solitary man. Among apostles there is no party-solidarity, not even theoretically; one apostle does not look at another apostle to see what he should do; each one is personally bound to God as a single individual. Thus the apostle confers and consults with God and with his conscience. Thereafter he opens the door, as it were, the door of his solitary enclosure, and goes, *mir nichts und dir nichts*,[7] with God out into the streets—in order to proclaim the Word. Suppose that someone meets him and says: Do you know that the Sanhedrin has stipulated flogging as punishment for preaching the Word? The apostle replies: Well, if the Sanhedrin has done that, then I shall be flogged. The next day the Sanhedrin imposes the death penalty. The apostle answers: Well, if the Sanhedrin has done that, then I shall be executed. He lets the established order stand—not a word, not a syllable, not a letter directed toward an external change, not the fleetingest thought in his head, not a blink of the eyelid, not a flicker of the countenance in this direction. "No," says the apostle, "just let the established order stand unshakably firm, for by the help of God it also stands unshakably firm that today I am flogged and tomorrow executed or—it amounts to the same thing—that today I proclaim the Word and tomorrow, Amen." Thank you, thank you, that you acted in this way. If you had acted as modern Christians do, Christianity would never have entered the world!

And here a Christian memento. Christianity within "Christendom" properly means, in self-concern, an indifference to externals. But if someone collides with the established order in such a way that he could imagine it to be a question of conscience—good God, a question of conscience!—and he dares to say it, then he has to be a solitary person in order to strive through suffering, in order to choose martyrdom. Conscience and a matter of conscience can be represented only through action by a solitary person and in character, by action,* not by prompting a discussion which is concluded

* Luther's marriage to Katharina von Bora can serve as an example—for with Luther there never was, no, with Luther there never was any nonsense.

How did he act? He counselled with God and with his conscience. After frightful struggling and spiritual trials [Anfægtelser] he came to this conclusion: At this point an intensive action must be ventured. This was a matter of conscience! He was silent. Although resolved, he remained silent. Then came the moment to act—he married. "A priest?!" Yes, in spite of the Pope. "With a nun?!" Yes, in spite of all public opinion.—Thank you. Do not disdain a grateful congratulatory message on your marriage—on that day you were hardly overwhelmed by congratulations! Do not disdain a congratulatory message because it is from a single man—it would perhaps be too much if you were to receive congratulations today from all the "married priests."

On the other hand, how did he not act? He did not go around with hearty nonsense to every Tom, Dick, and Harry, friends and acquaintances, casting a world-historical glance at the Church's past and ditto at its future. Nor did he talk to those "many friends" in this way: "The question of priests' marrying is a matter of conscience. But what are we to do? Let's get together, try to get a few more, and then I shall come out with a petition. Let's go to parliament. It is true that the matter concerns me on religious grounds, but there is a substantial party interested in the same thing for secular reasons. If we get together with them in the voting, according to my exact knowledge of numerical ratios (knowledge of numerical ratios—fix this in your memory, preserve it for the historian, for this phrase is the secret of my life—knowledge of numerical ratios is really what makes 'the reformer') it is not impossible, it is not impossible that we can squeeze a few points from the opposition and squeeze our way through—to freedom of conscience!—by a very scant simple majority. According to what I know about numerical ratios this is not at all impossible. And if it should develop that this cannot be achieved, we can withdraw the petition; therefore the matter is not dangerous at all." No, the matter certainly is not risky.—Forgive me, dear Luther, you man of God and man of spiritual trials, but I believe that however reluctant you would be to see such deportment you would nevertheless agree with me that there is really nothing more to do than to say: The matter is not dangerous at all. The only danger—and this would be very dangerous—the only danger would be that such a thing might be regarded as reformation and earnestness.

by voting—this is eternally certain and is rooted in the nature of the case. Everything which is partisan and wants to function as a party, perhaps even by intrigue—if it wants to appeal to "conscience" against an established order, is guilty of an untruth.

If it is a matter of conscience, it must be fought out in this way. If it is not a matter of conscience, then it becomes something entirely different. Christianity means precisely this: in self-concern to develop an indifference toward externals. However, if there is some change or other which a weaker person might desire (for, understood in this way, the stronger person is the very one who in self-concern has the greatest indifference), he then expresses this desire by saying: I could wish—but he does not speak of a matter of conscience, and he shudders at the thought that this should become "a habit" for him. This is my understanding, for I am a hater of "habitual Christianity."

Søren Kierkegaard

SELECTED ENTRIES
FROM THE
JOURNALS AND PAPERS

My position is armed neutrality.

II A 770   n.d., 1838

N.B.   N.B.

A new book ought to be written entitled: *Thoughts Which Cure Radically, Christian Healing.*

It will deal with the doctrine of the Atonement, showing first of all that the root of the sickness is sin. It will have two parts. Perhaps it is better to have three.

1. First comes: Thoughts which wound from behind—for up-building or edification. This will be the polemical element, something like "The Cares of the Pagans," but somewhat stronger, since Christian discourses should be given in quite a milder tone.

(1) [changed from (2)] On the Consciousness of Sin.
> *The Sickness unto Death*
> Christian Discourses

(2) [changed from (3)] *Radical Cure* [changed from: *Thoughts Which Cure Radically*]
> Christian Healing
> The Atonement

VIII¹ A 558   n.d., 1848

N.B.   N.B.

Wednesday, April 19

My whole nature is changed. My concealment and reserve [*Inde-sluttethed*][1] are broken—I am free to speak.

Great God, grant me grace!

It is true what my father said of me: "You will never amount to anything as long as you have money." He spoke prophetically; he thought I would lead a wild life. But not exactly that. No, but with my acumen and with my melancholy, and then to have money—O, what a propitious climate for developing all kinds of self-torturing torments in my heart.*

How marvellously timed—just when I had resolved to speak, my physician came. I did not, however, speak to him; it seemed too sudden. But my resolution remains firm—to speak.

Maundy Thursday and Good Friday have become true holy days for me.

VIII[1] A 640   April 19, 1848

* Alas, she could not break the silence of my melancholy. That I loved her[2]—nothing is more certain—and in this way my melancholy got enough to feed upon, O, it got a frightful extra measure.** That I became a writer was due essentially to her, my melancholy, and my money. Now, by the help of God, I shall become myself. I now believe that Christ will help me to triumph over my melancholy, and then I shall become a pastor.

In my melancholy I have still loved the world, for I loved my melancholy. Everything has been conducive to a higher tension of the relationship for me; her suffering, all my endeavor, and finally the fact that I have had to experience derision and now am brought to the point where I am obliged to earn a living have contributed with God's help to a break-through.

** And yet she could not become mine. I was and am a penitent and only got a frightfully intensified punishment through having entered into this relationship.

VIII[1] A 641   n.d., 1848

Saturday

I have just read Luther's sermon according to my reading plan;[3] it was the gospel about the ten lepers. O, Luther is still the master of us all.

VIII[1] A 642   April 22, 1848

N.B.   N.B.

Easter Monday

No, no, my reserve still cannot be broken, at least not now. The thought of wanting to break it continually occupies me so much and in such a way that it only becomes more and more chronic.

Yet I find some consolation in having talked with my physician. I have frequently been apprehensive about myself, that I might be too proud to speak to anyone. But just as I have done it before, so I have done it again. And what could a physician say, really? Nothing. But for me it is important to have had respect for this human authority.

My intellectual work satisfies me completely and makes me submit to everything gladly, if I only may give myself to it. I can understand my life in this way: that I declare consolation and joy to others while I am myself bound in a pain for which I can see no alleviation—except this, that I am able to work with my mind in this way. Ah, in this respect I truly cannot complain about the conditions of my life; on the contrary, I thank God every day that he has granted me much more than I ever expected; I pray every day that he will permit me to dare to thank him—this he knows.

But this was the situation. My future becomes more and more difficult economically. If I did not have this reticence to lug around, I could accept an appointment. Now it is difficult. I have long pondered the possibility of a break-through, and because hitherto I have operated essentially as an escapist, trying to forget, I have frequently thought it my duty to make an attempt to take the offensive, particularly since this reserve can become an occasion of sin for me.

Had I not done this, I should always have this to reproach me.

Now I have done it, and I understand myself again, better than before, for which this has been helpful.

Now I hope that God in some way or other will come to the aid of my work as a writer or will in other ways help me make a living and thus permit me to continue as a writer.

I do believe in the forgiveness of sins, but I interpret this, as before, to mean that I must bear my punishment of remaining in this painful prison of reserve all my life, in a more profound sense separated from the company of other men; yet this is mitigated by the thought that God has forgiven me. As yet, at least, I cannot come to such heights of faith, I cannot yet win such cheerful confidence of faith that I can believe that painful memory away. But in faith I protect myself against despair, bear the pain and punishment of my reserve—and am so indescribably happy or blessed in the activity of mind and spirit which God has granted to me so richly and graciously.

If my reserve is to be broken, it is perhaps more likely to happen in some way or other by God's helping me into an occupation and then helping me to concentrate fully on this. But to want to break a reserve formally by continually thinking about breaking it leads to the very opposite.

VIII[1] A 645   April 24, 1848

It was a miracle when Christ said to the paralytic: Your sins are forgiven, arise and walk.[4] But if that miracle does not happen to me now—what miraculous cheerfulness one's faith must have to believe that sin is entirely forgotten, so that memory of it brings no anguish, truly to believe this and to become a new man so that one hardly recognizes himself again!

VIII[1] A 646   n.d., 1848

But I am in need of physical recreation and rest. The proof-reading of the last book at such a time, spiritual trial [*Anfægtelse*] with regard to its publication, the economic question amid the difficulties of the times, seven years of continuous work, having to move, and now that even Anders[5] is being taken from me and I am all alone—yet constantly working and producing (thank God! This is the only thing that helps me. Even in these days I have written something on the new book about the sickness unto death)—all this has put me somewhat under a strain. I had counted on travelling considerably during the year—and now there is no place to travel to.

Out of all this a troubled spiritual trial—which nevertheless with God's help will help me and has helped me to understand myself better. God be praised; God is love—this, after all, is the happy side of my life, the up until now—God be praised—rejuvenating and continually renewing source of my joy.

More and more I understand that Christianity is really too blessed and beatific for us men. Just think what it means to dare to believe that God has come into the world also for my sake. Indeed, it almost sounds like the most blasphemous arrogance for a human being to dare presume to believe such a thing. If it were not God himself who had said it—if a human being had hit upon this in order to show the significance a human being has to God—it would be the most frightful blasphemy of all. But this is why it has not been invented to show how significant a human being is to God, but it is to show what infinite love God's love is. It is indeed infinite that he bothers about a sparrow, but to let himself be born and die for the sake of sinners (and a sinner is even less than a sparrow) —O, infinite love!

VIII[1] A 648   n.d., 1848

N.B.   N.B.

May 11, '48

Most men (if at an early age it is indicated that they must bear some suffering or other, some cross or other, one of those mournful curtailments of the soul) begin to hope and, as it is called, to have faith that everything will improve, that God will surely make everything all right etc., and then after a while, when still no change has taken place, they will learn little by little to depend on the help of the eternal—that is, resign themselves and be strengthened in being satisfied with the eternal.—The person of deeper nature or one whom God has structured [*anlagt*] more eternally begins at once to understand that he must bear this as long as he lives, that he dare not ask God for such extraordinary, paradoxical aid. But God is still perfect love, and nothing is more certain to him than that. Consequently he resigns himself, and since the eternal is close to him, he finds rest; continually and happily assured that God is love. But he must accept suffering. Then after a while when he becomes more and more concrete in the actuality [*Virkelighed*] of life, comes more and more to himself *qua* finite being, when time and the movement of time exercise their power over him, when in spite of all effort it still remains so difficult to live year after year with the aid only of the eternal, when in a more humble sense he becomes human or learns what it means to be a human being (for in his resignation he is still too ideal, too abstract, for which reason there is some despair in all resignation)—then for him faith's possibility means: will he believe or not that by virtue of the absurd God will help him temporally.* (Here lie all the paradoxes. Thus the forgiveness of sins means to be helped temporally; otherwise it is resignation, which can endure the punishment, still assured that God is love. But belief in the forgiveness of sins means to believe that in time God has forgotten the sin, that it is really true that God forgets.)

This is to say that most men never reach faith at all. They live a long time in immediacy or spontaneity, finally they advance to some reflection, and then they die. The exceptions begin the other way around; dialectical from childhood, that is, without immediacy, they begin with the dialectical, with reflection, and they go on living this way year after year (about as long as the others live in sheer immediacy) and then, at a more mature age, faith's possibility presents itself to them. For faith is immediacy or spontaneity after reflection.[6]

Naturally the exceptions have a very unhappy childhood and youth, for to be essentially reflective at that age, which by nature is spontaneous or immediate, is the most profound melancholy.

But there is a return. Most people drift on in such a way they never become spirit; all their many happy years of immediacy tend toward spiritual retardation and therefore they never become spirit. But the unhappy childhood and youth of the exceptions are transfigured into spirit.

* Note. This is the inverse movement, which after all is "spirit." Spirit is the second movement. Humor is not mood but is found, with dialectical propriety, in a person who unhappily has been cheated of his childhood and then later becomes spirit and simultaneously aware of childhood.

VIII[1] A 649   May 11, 1848

*   *
*

It is wonderful how God's love overwhelms me still—alas, when all is said and done I know of no truer prayer than the one I pray over and over, that God will tolerate me, that he will not become angry with me because I continually thank him for having done and for doing so indescribably much more for me than I had ever anticipated. Encompassed by derision, plagued day in and day out by the pettiness of men, yes, even those closest to me, I know of nothing else to do in private or in my innermost being but to thank and thank God, because I comprehend that what he has done for me is indescribable. A human being—and after all what is a human being before God, a nothing, less than nothing—and then a poor human being who from childhood on has fallen into the most miserable melancholy, an object of anxiety to himself—and then God helps in this way and grants to me what he has granted to me! A life which was a burden to me however much I knew at times all the happy strains, which was all embittered by the black spot that spoiled everything, a life which, if others knew its secret, I perceived would make me an object of pity and sympathy from the very outset and a burden to myself—God takes a life like that under his wing. He allows me to weep before him in quiet solitude, to empty and again empty out my pain, blessedly consoled by the knowledge that he is concerned for me—and at the same time he gives this life of pain a significance which almost overwhelms me, grants me success and power and wisdom for all my efforts to make my whole existence a pure expression of ideas, or he himself makes it into that.

For now I see so clearly (again unto new joy in God, a new occasion to give thanks) that my life has been planned. My life began without spontaneity or immediacy [*Umiddelbarhed*], with a frightful melancholy, basically disturbed from earliest childhood, a melancholy which plunged me into sin and dissipation for a time, and yet, humanly speaking, almost more deranged than guilty. Then my father's death really stopped me. I did not dare to believe that this, the fundamental wretchedness of my being, could be lifted; so I grasped the eternal, blessedly assured that God is love indeed, even though I should have to suffer in this way all my life, yes, blessedly assured of this. This is the way I regarded my life. Then once again I was plunged down, also sympathetically, into the abyss of my melancholy by having to break off my engagement— and why?—simply because I dared not believe that God would lift the elemental misery of my being, take my almost deranged melancholy away, something I now desired with all the passion of my whole soul for her sake and also for mine. It was most grievous to have to reproduce my own misery. Once again I resigned myself. Thinking only of working her free, I moved towards such a life, but always assured and blessedly assured, God be praised, that God is love—nothing has been more certain to me.

And now, now when in many ways I have been brought to the breaking point, now (since last Easter, although with intermissions), a hope has awakened in my soul that it may still be God's will to lift this elemental misery of my being. That is, I now believe in the deepest sense. Faith is spontaneity after reflection. As poet and philosopher I have presented everything in the medium of imagination, myself living in resignation. Now life draws nearer to me, or I draw nearer to myself, come to myself.—For God all things are possible. This thought is now in the deepest sense my watchword and has gained a meaning for me which I had never envisioned. Just because I see no way out, I must never have the audacity to say that therefore there is none for God. For it is despair and blasphemy to confuse one's own little crumb of imagination and the like with the possibilities God has at his disposal.

VIII¹ A 650   n.d., 1848
[Between entries dated May 11, 1848,
and May 13, 1848, in Journal NB⁴.]

Something about the Forgiveness of Sins

To believe the forgiveness of one's sins is the decisive crisis whereby a human being becomes spirit; he who does not believe this is not spirit.[7] Maturity of the spirit means that spontaneity is completely lost, that a person is not only capable of nothing by himself but is capable only of injury to himself. But how many in truth come in a wholly personal way to understand about themselves that one is brought to this extremity. (Here lies the absurd, offense, the paradox, forgiveness of sins.)

Most men never become spirit, never experience becoming spirit. The stages—child, youth, adult, oldster—they pass through these with no credit to themselves; it is none of their doing, for it is a vegetative or vegetative-animal process. But they never experience becoming spirit.

The forgiveness of sins is not a matter of particulars—as if on the whole one were good (this is childish, for the child always begs forgiveness for some particular thing which he did yesterday and forgets today, etc.; it could never occur to a child, in fact, the child could not even get into his head, that he is actually evil); no, it is just the opposite—it pertains not so much to particulars as to the totality; it pertains to one's whole self, which is sinful and corrupts everything as soon as it comes in slightest contact with it.

Anyone who in truth has experienced and experiences what it is to believe the forgiveness of one's sins has indeed become another person. Everything is forgotten—but still it is not with him as with the child who, after having received pardon, becomes essentially the same child again. No, he has become an eternity older, for he has now become spirit. All spontaneity and its selfishness, its selfish attachment to the world and to himself, have been lost. Now he is, humanly speaking, old, very old, but eternally he is young.

VIII[1] A 673   n.d., 1848

We ought not despise the leap.[8] There is something extraordinary in it. Therefore among almost all peoples there is a legend about a leap whereby the innocent are saved, whereas the evil are plunged into the abyss—a leap which only the innocent can perform.

VIII[1] A 681   n.d., 1848

Luther is entirely right in naming these among the marks of the Christian (No. 7): they (Christians) inwardly sorrow and are grieved, are agonized and yet do not give up, but outwardly they are poor, despised, sick, frail, so that in all things they may become like their master Christ, may share and receive the blessing he promises all who suffer persecution for his name's sake.

See Rudelbach, *Biographier*, the article on Jesper Swedberg, p. 553.[9]

IX A 7   n.d., 1848

If I should need a new pseudonym in the future, he shall be called Anticlimacus.[10] And then he must be recklessly ironical and humorous.

IX A 9   n.d., 1848

I understand very well how I ought to conduct myself in order to be understood—honored and esteemed—how I could gain these benefits even by preaching Christianity. But this is simply unchristian—that the one who preaches Christianity is not himself what he says is Christianity. Christ has not inaugurated assistant-professors—but imitators:[11] Follow me. It is not *cogito ergo sum*—but the opposite, *sum ergo cogito*. It is not: I think self-renunciation, therefore I am self-renouncing; but if I truly am self-renouncing, then I must certainly have also thought self-renunciation.

The one who preaches Christianity shall therefore (he *shall*, it is something he has to take care of himself) himself be just as polemical as that which he preaches.

IX A 49   n.d., 1848

. . . . . Thus in a certain sense I began my activity as an author with a *falsum* or with a pious fraud. The situation is that in so-called established Christendom men are so fixed in the fantasy that they are Christian that if they are to be made aware at all many an art will have to be employed. If someone who does not have a reputation of being an author begins right off as a Christian author, he will not get a hearing from his contemporaries. They are immediately on their guard, saying, "That's not for us" etc.

I began as an estheticist—and then, although approaching the religious with perhaps uncustomary alacrity, I denied being a Christian, and so on.

This is the way I present myself as an author to my contemporaries—and in any case this is the way I belong to history. My thought is that here I am permitted and able to speak of myself only as an author. I do not believe that my personality, my personal life, and what I consider my shortcomings are of any concern to the public. I am an author, and who I am and what my endowments are I know well enough. I have submitted to everything that could serve my cause.

I ask the more competent ones in particular to be slow to judge the capabilities and the use of capabilities which do not appear every day—I ask this especially of the more competent, for there is no use in requesting this of fools. But as a rule every more competent person has respect for himself and for his judgments—and for just this reason I request him to judge carefully.

It is Christianity that I have presented and still want to present; to this every hour of my day has been and is directed.

IX A 171   n.d., 1848

In margin of IX A 171:

It was essential for me to learn to know the age. Perhaps the age found it quite easy to form a picture of this author: that he was an exceptionally intellectually gifted person dedicated to pleasure and wallowing in a life of luxury. Ah, it was mistaken. It never dreamed that the author of *Either/Or* had said goodbye to the world long before, that he spent much of the day in fear and trembling reading edifying books, in prayer and supplication. Least of all did it think that he was and is conscious of himself as a penitent from the very first line he wrote.[12]

IX A 172   n.d., 1848

In margin: See this journal, p. 18 [i.e., IX A 171, 172].

Presumably it would be the right thing at some time to give my contemporaries a definite and non-reduplicated[13] idea of what I myself mean, what I am aiming at, etc. This is what I have in mind as the program of *Armed Neutrality*, a periodical, which should come out simultaneously with the second edition of *Either/Or*. In it I would scrutinize Christianity piece by piece and get the coil spring set in place.

From the very first I have dedicated myself to and belonged to the cause of Christianity. It will always be important to Christianity to have someone who logs the course to see where we are and whether the whole thing has not run aground in an illusion, someone who presents Christianity quite recklessly, yet without attacking Tom, Dick, or Harry, but leaving it up to each one to test himself.

The trouble, however, is that by using direct communication I win men over—and consequently weaken the truth. The confusion in Christendom is so great at this point (that is, Christianity has been abolished) that in order to open people's eyes it is necessary for someone to be put to death openly for sake of the cause.

But as soon as I use direct communication my own situation will be eased, and, on the other hand, where will I find anyone to serve the truth under the most stringent conditions. I know of no one, literally no one. This is not arrogance; it is an awkward situation for me; I am a penitent who in fear and trembling must be willing to humble myself under everything.

O, how easy it must be to place oneself at the head of a few people, and then thousands, and make a big noise—and then leave the truth in the lurch, although one fancies himself to be serving it and is honored for doing so. My method is slower.

What makes it all so difficult is the torment that the future may make it necessary for me to throw everything overboard in order to make a living. I can see my way out of all the other pressures—but to have this worry on top of everything else!

Yet it is good for me that I do nothing rash but really stand in need of God in every way.

The minute I use direct communication, the truth loses its intensity and I to some extent escape martyrdom: is this permissible, is this not deceiving God? If it is thinkable that after my death the indirect communication will give a quite different momentum to the truth I have had the honor to serve, is it not my duty to keep on using it? On the other hand, may it not be pride and arrogance not to want to use direct communication? But have I not provided enough to be understood by any earnest person who is willing to understand? Yes, before God I dare affirm this.

This is where the matter stands, now that I have turned over in my mind the possibility of imminent death and that the crucial works will be published after my death.

In truth, I am heavily armed, but with all this I cannot thank God sufficiently for all the good he has done for me, so indescribably much more than I had expected.

As for now, I shall work calmly under God on the book about offense which I am writing, confident that God will give me a certain spirit. My personal life also demands its time—that in all this enormous work I do not forget the one thing needful—to sorrow over my own sins. This thought can clear the air immediately—and drive out all notions of importance.

                                        IX A 212   n.d., 1848

It was a good thing that I published that little article[14] and came under tension. If I had not published it, I would have gone on living in a certain ambiguity about the future use of indirect communication.

Now it is clear to me that henceforth it will be indefensible to use it.

The awakening effect is rooted in God's having given me power to live as a riddle—but not any longer, lest the awakening effect end by being confusing.

The thing to do now is to take over unambiguously the maieutic structure of the past, to step forth definitely and directly in character, as one who has wanted and wants to serve the cause of Christianity.

If I had not published that little article, indirect communication would have continued to hover vaguely before me as a possibility and I would not have gotten the idea that I dare not use it.

I dare not say of myself that I have had a clear panorama of the whole plan of production from the outset; I must rather say, as I have continually acknowledged, that I myself have been brought up or educated and developed in the process of my work, that personally I have become committed more and more to Christianity than I was. Nevertheless this remains fixed, that I began with the deepest religious impression, alas, yes, I who when I began bore the tremendous responsibility of the life of another human being and understood it as God's punishment upon me.

                                        IX A 218   n.d., 1848

The thought that I would soon die,[15] the thought in which I have rested, has now been disturbed by the publication of that little article; it would disturb me if this were to be the last thing I publish.

But on the other hand the thought of dying now was only a gloomy notion[16]—how good then that I published that little article. This very thing had to be probed—and the publication of the article served to do this.

IX A 219   n.d., 1848

In margin of IX A 219:
But in my case there is R. Nielsen[17] as one who can provide explanation.

IX A 220   n.d., 1848

Yet the communication of the essentially Christian must end finally in "witnessing." The maieutic cannot be the final form,[18] because, Christianly understood, the truth does not lie in the subject (as Socrates understood it), but in a revelation which must be proclaimed.

It is very proper that the maieutic be used in Christendom, simply because the majority actually live in the fancy that they are Christians. But since Christianity still is Christianity, one who uses the maieutic must become a witness.

Ultimately the user of the maieutic will be unable to bear the responsibility, for the maieutic approach still remains rooted in human sagacity, however sanctified and dedicated in fear and trembling this may be. God becomes too powerful for the maieutic practitioner and then he is a witness, different from the direct witness only in what he has gone through to become a witness.

IX A 221   n.d., 1848

Add the thought of death to the publication of that little article! If I had died without it—well, anyone could publish my posthumous papers, and in any case R. Nielsen would be there. But the illusion that I did not become a religious author until I was old and perhaps on the basis of accidentals still· would have been pos-

sible. Now, however, the dialectical breaks are clear: *Either/Or* and
two edifying discourses, *Concluding Postscript*, two years of edifying works,[19] and then a little esthetic essay.[20]

IX A 228   n.d., 1848

Unqualified indirect communication belongs to being more than
human, and no man, therefore, has the right to use it. The God-
man cannot do otherwise, because he is qualitatively different from
man. In paganism it is demonic, but this has no place in Christendom.

As soon as a person is decisively, personally Christian, he dares
not carry the dialectical so high that he posits the possibility of offense. The God-man cannot do otherwise, simply because he is the
object of faith.

In paganism, therefore, the abstract indirect method could certainly be used, for the possibility of offense was not present. And
also thus in relation to Christendom (which is very far from being
purely Christian, but is closer to paganism) [it may be used] by one
who has not unconditionally stepped forth as personally being
Christian in a decisive sense. For where the proportions are such
as these, offense cannot become more than a kind of awakening.

IX A 260   n.d., 1848

I am still very exhausted, but I have also almost reached the goal.
The work *The Point of View for My Work as an Author* is now as
good as finished. Relying upon what I have done in the past to support my productivity, in the recent period I have been only a writer.
My mind and spirit is strong enough, but regrettably all too strong
for my body.[21] In one sense it is my mind and spirit which helps me
to endure such poor health; in another sense it is my mind and
spirit which overwhelms my body.

IX A 293   n.d., 1848

N.B.

Perhaps it would be best to publish all the last four books ("The

Sickness unto Death," "Come Hither," "Blessed Is He Who Is Not Offended," "Armed Neutrality") in one volume under the title
                    Collected Works of Completion
                 [*Fuldendelsens samtlige Værker*]*
with "The Sickness unto Death" as Part I. The second part would be called "An Attempt to Introduce Christianity into Christendom" and below: poetic—without authority. "Come Hither" and "Blessed Is He Who Is Not Offended" would be entered as subdivisions. Perhaps there could also be a third part, which I am now writing,** but in that case Discourse No. 1 would be a kind of introduction which is not counted.

   And then it should be concluded.

   In margin:
   * Perhaps rather:
   Collected Works of Consummation [*Fuldbringelsens*]
and the volume should be quarto.
   ** "From on High He Will Draw All Men unto Himself."
   The three: "Come Hither," "Blessed Is He Who Is Not Offended," and "From on High," would then have a separate title-page: *Attempt to Introduce Christianity into Christendom*, but at the bottom of the title-page: poetic attempt—without authority.

                                        IX A 390   n.d., 1848

   If there were any question about my having gone a little bit too far out (that is, I have not gone far out yet; it is still in my power to turn aside, but I consider the possibility of going that far out), then it would be with regard to the necessity of suffering, of succumbing, i.e., that I do not remain in suspension, leaving it to a still uncertain determination whether or not I am just as likely to win out or at least come out somehow, etc.

   The situation is that the ideal must necessarily suffer, succumb, become a sacrifice in this world; here is the unconditional necessity, for in relationship to the ideal the circumstances of existence [*Tilværelses*] can be calculated purely dialectically. But no human being is sheer ideality or the ideal, and of course I am not that at all. For this very reason there has been for me the possibility of variation with respect to the outcome of my striving—but this is obviously no perfection on my part; it is my imperfection.

Moreover, the ideal does nothing at all in order to enter into suffering, for suffering comes necessarily because it is the ideal—and because it must be in the world of reality. However, if an individual human being who is not the ideal were to think that he should do nothing at all in order to enter into suffering (i.e., to venture), perhaps in order not to tempt God—then existence cannot get hold of him, that is, cannot test him in spiritual trial [*Anfægtelse*], for spiritual trial is precisely the suffering of the voluntary or the suffering of whether one has not ventured too much.

IX A 392   n.d., 1848

Conclusion

In margin: Possibly better used in the opening of the conclusion, in which case the two first portions drop out.

The present work[22] is a *conception* of something past, something put aside, something *historical*. Thus in a way it belongs itself to the past; therefore a good deal more might be said, something which I should prefer not to have to say but which *historically* ought not and cannot be forgotten or suppressed.

This is now completed; the historical truth gets its due by way of a *direct* communication, but—and this of course does not belong to the past—for this very reason my whole relationship as an author is altered. The accounting has been made; on the other hand, with the direct communication contained in this work, I have abandoned the mode of polemical subtlety—it would be a contradiction to want to be subtle and direct at the same time.

This means, in order to bring the introduction to mind at the conclusion, to come out with it as definitely, as directly, as openly, as reconcilingly, as amicably as possible. Since I now regard it as my religious duty to speak, with God's help I shall speak honestly in this spirit and to the best of my ability. My heart expands—not that it has ever beaten constrictedly within me, but the inwardness which has been in my life, and which I thought would be my death, now gets air—the dialectical bonds are loosened; I dare speak directly. . . .

IX B 57   n.d., 1848

"Upbringing" is the one thing needful:* there must once again be upbringing in Christianity. But "the race" cannot "be brought up" in Christianity; this is just as impossible as adding disparate quantities. "To bring up" is not commensurate with "the race" and "to bring up the race" is not commensurate with Christianity. "To bring up the human race" veritably means to transform "the human race" into "the single individuals" in order to begin "upbring-

* Note. Parenthetically, no one can know this better than I do, I who have always reckoned my principal advantage among my contemporaries to be that I have been well brought up in Christianity from childhood. Again, no one can know this better than I, whose entire activity as an author, at least from one point of view, can be regarded as a reflection of the author's having been brought up rigorously in Christianity and then educated once again.

In margin: So that at least from one point of view I, the author, am myself the one who has been educated. Therefore I, the author, if I think of being in relation to the age, am far from calling myself the educator—no, I myself am the one who has been educated or brought up. This is one of the reasons I have been so scrupulous about avoiding admiration, adherents, cheers, and other hoopla, for, good heavens, there is no point in shouting hurrah because someone is brought up and one certainly does not become an adherent of—a disciple. On the other hand this is one of the reasons I have been willing to submit to all the very opposite; like a volunteer I have even risked becoming, alas, the poor "master of irony"!—becoming a sacrifice to laughter—all of which is connected with being brought up, and one who is to be brought up and is willing can benefit greatly from it.

By God's help and with wise teachers, one learns wisdom *directly* in the first lesson. The person who, in order to go through such a course, ventures into the second lesson and does not become a distracted but an attentive, diligent, hard-working, obedient pupil, learns profound wisdom from God through having had the courage to expose himself to fools as his teachers.

ing," because "single individuals" are brought up, or "single individuals" are "brought up in Christianity."

But if there is to be "upbringing" in Christianity—and the stage is not the hidden enclosure of family life or the fenced-in school yard or the peaceful security of the Church, where the educator has the upper hand, but the stage is historical actuality, where the educator is weakest, weakest of all—what is the educator called here? He is not called "priest" or "parish clerk" or even "professor," although he may possibly have these names, too, but essentially he is called "the martyr." On the stage of historical actuality the martyr brings up or educates in Christianity, and since it is in "Christendom," where all are Christians, he consequently educates Christians in Christianity. Through his own obedience he teaches obedience. He is not a teacher who teaches by beating the pupils; the main characteristic of his teaching is to teach by letting himself be beaten. The learners do not, I dare say, get his agreement and consent, but they do get the permission of his patience and thus have leave to do with him as they will. Finally they put him to death—and now the real instruction begins, now they learn obedience from him, or from their having put him to death.

IX B 63:11   n.d., 1848

"The martyr" ("the missionary") will by all means have within himself what is appropriate to the age, "the age of reflection"—an infinite reflection as a servant in respect to becoming a martyr, so that, knowing the times from the bottom up, he succeeds in falling at the right spot and assures that his death wounds come in the right spot. This superior reflection and this infinitely reflected work of reflection in *becoming* a martyr will constitute his distinction from all earlier martyrs, from the martyr of immediacy who simply required the faith and courage to risk his life but perhaps did not need it over a long period, in any case did not need the extremely complicated labor of reflection involved in dialectically determining the place where he shall fall. Whole volumes could be written about this alone.

IX B 63:12   n.d., 1848

This category [the single individual],[23] to have used this category, and furthermore, to have used it so decisively and personally— this is the decisive factor. Without this category and without the use made of it, reduplication would be lacking. Just because everything present in the works had been said, presented, taught, developed, and enthusiastically expressed and perhaps with imagination, dialectic, psychological insight, etc.—from this it would by no means directly follow that the author had understood (and had known how to express absolutely decisively in a single word that he had understood his age and himself in it) that it *was an age of disintegration.** That it was an age of disintegration, an esthetic, effeminate disintegration, so that before there could be any question even of merely introducing the religious the ethically strengthening either/or had to precede. That it was an age of disintegration, that "the system" itself (according to which this author pushes forward in historical sequence), like overripe fruit, was a sign of decline and did not, as the systematicians self-complacently interpreted it, signify that perfection was now attained. That it was an age of disintegration and therefore not, as the politicians thought, a matter of the "government" being evil, which would have been a curious self-contradiction for the viewpoint "the single individual," but that the crowd, the public, was the evil,** which coincides with the viewpoint, the single individual. That it was an age of disintegration, that it was not nationalities which should be advanced but Christianity, and a Christianity relating to the single individual, that no particular class could be the stake but "the crowd," and that the task is to make it into individuals. That it was an age of disintegration, a critical time when history is about to take a turn, that

* Note. And now in '48!
** Note. And now in '48 this is no doubt understood.

it was a matter of having heard right, of being in propitious rapport with the times and the turn which should be made—that it was the ethical that should be accented, but above all that the ethical should not be systematically muddled up or conglomerated with the old order, consequently that it was not simply a question of teaching the ethical objectively but of denoting the ethical, of ethically putting into action the qualitative force of the ethical, "the single individual," and in a measure to support it by personal existing (again in qualitative distinction to system, objective instruction, and everything related), yet consistently to continue for the time being to hide in the careful incognito of a _"flaneur."_ This puts the productivity over into another sphere, for "that single individual" will become an historic point of view.—This is why I do not call myself a "witness to the truth." By this I do not mean everyone who says something true. In that sense, thank you, we have enough witnesses to the truth. No, in a witness to the truth there must be a relationship between personal existing and what is said. The word "witness" refers to personal life—a reference which, it is quite true, the system and objective teaching and the characterlessness of the age have abolished completely. My life has no doubt scrupulously expressed the ethical, has ethically accentuated being the single individual. I have associated with innumerable people, but I have always stood alone, unconditionally alone. For the sake of this, my category, I have also ventured in various ways, offered more than one sacrifice, exposed myself to more than one danger— and, mind you, to the kind of danger which is categorically appropriate to being "the single individual"—exposed myself to the "crowd," the "public," to gossip and laughter. But even though there were no other hindrance, I do have an inheritance. Just that is enough; therefore I do not call myself a witness to the truth; this is a benefit which places me down in a lower category. But in addition I have also had too much imagination and been too much of a poet to dare be called a witness to the truth in the strict sense; moreover, I have been far from grasping the whole thing clearly

from the beginning but have been aided both by a fortunate spontaneity and by providence, which at more than one point have
helped me spontaneously to go the right way; thus the productivity
has also been my own development and I have learned progres-
sively to understand that I have gone the right way. I have been
involved in the ethical too much to be a poet, but I am too much
of a poet to be a witness to the truth; I am a *confinium* in between.
My function is to point to the highest. I am neither the one awaited
nor the forerunner of the one awaited, but a presentient person
who nevertheless with categorical exactitude has been related to
the historical future, to the turn which should be made and which
will become the future of history. It will go with me as with all
such figures—the very thing for which my contemporaries rejected
me and were angry with me, precisely that, word-for-word, will
become my eulogy in the future: he is eccentric, refractory, and
proud; he will not reduce the price, will not compromise.—This was
the charge, and the eulogy will read the same, word-for-word: he
would not reduce the price, he would not compromise. Integrity
of character always affronts the egotism of contemporaries, who,
opposing such a person, do not think of becoming informed about
him but only want to have power over him. The future, which is
interested only in the idea and not in personal externalities, will
find no affront in the fact that there lived a thinker who was consistent; on the contrary, the future will regard this as magnificent,
although, of course, in its own capacity of the contemporary public
it will behave like every contemporary public.

IX B 64   n.d., 1848

Addition to IX B 64:

That it is an age of disintegration—a dizziness occasioned by and
in a mounting fever fomented by constantly wanting with finite
cleverness to influence by means of numbers, to augment the moment by means of the momentary, and with the impatience of the
moment demanding to see the result at the moment—a situation

which only leads (if this is possible) to making it appallingly evident that what is needed is the very opposite: the eternal and the single individual.

IX B 65   n.d., 1848

Sharpened
a Double-edged Weapon

In times of peace the category "the single individual" is the category of awakening; when everything is peaceful, secure, and indolent—and the ideal has vanished—then the single individual is the awakening power. In agitated times, when everything is tottering, the single individual is the category of reassurance. In times of peace the person who knows how to use this category will appear quite different than in agitated times, and yet he will be using the same weapon, the difference being similar to using the same sharp instrument for wounding and using it at another time for cleaning out a wound. Rightly used, this category, "the single individual," will never be damaging to the existing order. Used in a time of peace its purpose will be to awaken inwardness unto heightened life in the established order without making any external change; and in agitated times its purpose will be to support the established order more directly by leading the single individual to be indifferent to external change and thus to support the established order. Earthly reward, power, honor, and the like can never be associated with the proper application of this category, because what is rewarded in the world is, of course, only external changes and working for external changes. Inwardness does not interest the world.

IX B 66   n.d., 1848

Armed Neutrality

See journal NB[11], p. 157 [i.e., x^1 A 450, p. 87 below].

If the three works [three parts of *Training in Christianity*] remain together under the title *Training in Christianity—An Essay*, this

[*Armed Neutrality*] can follow as an appendix, but of course pseudonymously and under the same pseudonym [Anti-Climacus]; in any case it must be published pseudonymously.

Addition: Written at the end of '48 or the beginning of '49. If I remember rightly this piece was written in '49 just after "From on High He Will Draw All Men unto Himself" [Part III of *Training in Christianity*].

x^5 B 105   n.d., 1849

Armed Neutrality
or
My Position as a Christian Author in Christendom

Appendix

to "The Point of View for My Work as an Author"
by
S. Kierkegaard

x^5 B 106   n.d., 1849

Armed Neutrality
or
My Position as a Christian
Author in Christendom

(Appendix to "The Point of View for My Work as an Author")
by
S. Kierkegaard

Draft
x^5 B 108   n.d., 1849

Addition to x⁵ B 108:

Armed Neutrality
or My Position as a Christian Author in Christendom

It is said that to remain in secular life is a higher form than to enter a monastery, but does it follow from this that every one who remains in secular life has made the monastic movement?*

But through science and scholarship, confusing also in life, we have left out as abrogated the whole dialectical element in connection with being a Christian, and thus being a Christian has been abolished. For example, the monastic movement (actual renunciation of the world) has thus been made a merely abrogated movement; we lie in saying that everyone in quietness, in his inner being, has done this—and then we return to the secularized life.

Let me try to make myself even clearer with regard to what this armed neutrality means.

---

* *Along margin:* But if this dialectic is not true, what it amounts to is not a return to secular life but outright secular-mindedness; the dialectic is so far from being resolved that it has not even been started.

x⁵ B 109   n.d., 1849

Addition to x⁵ B 108:

> The title could be: "Armed Neutrality, my standpoint as the editor of some pseudonymous writings, of which I am the stated editor." (Then this pertains to both *The Sickness unto Death* and Joh. Climacus.)

The work *Armed Neutrality* could perhaps be added to Anti-Climacus's *Training in Christianity* but as an appendix by the editor, therefore by me.

Then it would have to be retouched. At the very beginning it should read: Although I am only the editor of these writings, I well perceive that I do have a responsibility and that it is quite in order for me to give an account of my standpoint.

All the tenses would then have to be in the past and none in the future concerning what I intend to do; and so on.

x⁵ B 110   n.d., 1849

. . . I have another concern regarding *The Point of View for My Work as an Author*: that in some way I might have said too much about myself, or whether in some way God might want me to be silent about something. On the first point I have emphasized as decisively as possible in *A Cycle of Ethical-Religious Essays* that I am without authority; furthermore it is stated in the book that I am a penitent, that my entire activity as an author is my own upbringing or education, that I am *like* a spy in a higher service. Finally, in *Armed Neutrality*, every misunderstanding, as if I were an apostle, has been forestalled as decisively as possible. . . .

x¹ A 74, pp. 58-59   n.d., 1849

N.B.   N.B.
N.B.

Most of my concern that the completed works might put me in a false light as the extraordinary and the like is sheer hypochondria. As far as *A Cycle of Ethical-Religious Essays* is concerned, on looking through it again, I find it entirely in order. From the outset I have marked the other works: poetic attempt—without authority. In addition, *Armed Neutrality* contains this as scrupulously as possible.

The question, therefore, is on the other side: to what extent, after all, do I have the right to hold these works back.

In one sense I would prefer to be free, I would prefer to be free and to send them out into the world, just as if I suddenly had no responsibility to desist from sending them out.

x¹ A 97   n.d., 1849

Just as the Guadalquivir River plunges into the earth somewhere and then comes out again, so I must now plunge into pseudonymity, but I also understand now how I will emerge again under my own name. The important thing left is to do something about seeking an appointment and then travel.

(1) The three small ethical-religious treatises[24] will be anonymous; this was the earlier stipulation. (2) *The Sickness unto Death* will be anonymous and is to be gone through so that my name and the like are not in it. (3) The three works, "Come Hither All Ye," "Blessed Is He Who Is Not Offended," and "From on High He Will Draw All Men unto Himself" will be pseudonymous. Either all three in one volume under the common title, *Training in Christianity*, Essay by ————, or each one separately. They are to be checked so that my name and anything about me etc. are excluded, which is the case with number three. (4) Everything under the titles *The Point of View for My Work as an Author, A Note, Three Notes*, and *Armed Neutrality** cannot conceivably be published.

These writings properly remain pseudonymous. Here there is the dialectical tension and tightening with respect to the doctrine of sin and redemption, and then I begin with my own name in a simple edifying discourse. But it is one thing for a work of such a dialectical nature to appear pseudonymously and something quite different if it appears over my name, in character, as the finale of the whole effort.

After all, there is no hurry about publishing. But if it is to be in character and as a finale, it must be done as soon as possible, something which has pained me frightfully and which has now become almost an impossibility, because today, June 4, I spoke with Reitzel, who said he dared not take on anything new for publication. On the whole the man has plagued me unbearably with his miseries, which perhaps are exaggerated anyway.

A battle of ideas has taken place here. In actuality the whole matter of publishing with or without my name perhaps would have been a bagatelle. But to me in my ideality it is a very taxing problem so that above all I do not falsely hold myself back or falsely go too far but in truth understand myself and continue to be myself.

---

* See this journal, p. 157 [i.e., X1 A 450, p. 87 below].

I have struggled and suffered fearfully. Yet one who fights for the "You shall" as I do must also suffer at this point. But yet at times I probably have not been far from pressing this "You shall" in an almost melancholy-maniacal way. But now I understand myself. You shall—this is eternally true—but it is not less true and it is also a "You shall" that with God you shall understand your limits and beyond them you shall not go or you shall abandon such desires.

But, gracious God, how I have suffered and how I have struggled. Yet it is my consolation that the God of love will let this be to my good, and in a certain sense it consoles me that I have endured this suffering, because in this very suffering I have become convinced of the way I am to turn.

My misfortune always has been that it is so difficult for me to take an appointment. My melancholy, which is almost a quiet derangement, has been a hindrance to me all along, my consciousness of sin, too. This has aided me continually in venturing, for it has assured me that I was at least not being guided by vanity and the like. But now in God's name I must turn in this direction.

Strangely enough, incidentally, I have written so much in journal NB¹⁰ [i.e., X¹ A 82-294] and in this journal [NB¹¹, X¹ A 295-541], but there is on a loose sheet something I have not wished to enter in the journal and which I still really regard as the most decisive [factor] and also one of the earliest—I now end with precisely this.

X^1 A 422   June 4, 1849

> This is the loose sheet mentioned on page 129 of this journal [X¹ A 422]. To be written transversely in the journal.

If I had the means, I would venture further out—of course, not with the intention of being put to death (for this, after all, is sinful), but nevertheless, with this possibility in mind, believing that eventually my life might take a still higher turn.

Now I cannot, and I cannot defend venturing in the way which would give my life such a turn that I would really not recognize myself; whereas I fully recognize myself in the kind of persecution, if it may be called that, which I have suffered. Yes, from earliest childhood I have had the presentiment in my soul that things would turn out this way for me, that in a certain sense I should be regarded even with a certain solemnity as somewhat extraordinary and yet be laughed at and regarded as a bit mad.

Now I cannot. Now all my original plans go against me: to be a writer for only a few years and then seek an appointment, to practice the art of being able to stop—all the more so since it was my intention, never as definite as last year when I sold the house and made a little on it, to stop in earnest (I did not even rent rooms; this I did only much later) and to travel; and the Friday-discourses have always seemed to me to be a suitable terminating point. Perhaps I should have done that. I suffered much in '48, but I also learned much and in that case [travelling] I would scarcely have learned to know myself in this way.

Now I cannot. Suddenly to be forced to sustain a very perceptible financial loss, perhaps at a time when I am about to take the most decisive step—and then perhaps not to be put to death anyway and then to bungle the whole cause and myself—no, that I cannot do. To my mind it would be tempting God if I, spoiled by having had financial means, were now, with this new danger, to venture to a degree previously untried.

In addition, I now have a misgiving about myself which I would not have if I had financial means: is there possibly a connection between this almost martyr-impatience of mine and another kind of impatience, my shrinking from the humiliating task of actively seeking an appointment and from the humiliation implicit in all such things and in the whole mode of life? Moreover, I do have perhaps a trace of life-weariness. Perhaps it is also an exaggeration in the direction of expressing that I have suffered injustice and therefore could wish that they would put me to death.

Finally, there is a big question whether I, with my particular mental and spiritual capacities, am not intended to live, because the more there is of scientific scholarship and the like, the less relevant it is to work in this way.

Finally, it is part of being human not to become the very highest which one has envisioned—patience and humility in this respect. But a man will be wounded by this highest, and that I have been, through having been so close to it in thought.

Consequently I do not take the least little step in that direction.

x¹ A 424   n.d., 1849

Armed Neutrality can best be published as an appendix when the three works²⁵ are published as one (*Training in Christianity*, an Essay), but of course pseudonymously under the same pseudonym.

A pseudonym is excellent for accentuating a point, a stance, a position. It creates a poetic person. Therefore it is not as if I personally said: This is what I am fighting for—which indeed could become a duty for almost my entire life but which external conditions could make it impossible for me to fulfill, if, for example, I find it necessary to use most of my time to work for a living.

x¹ A 450   n.d., 1849

. . . Until now I have been a poet, absolutely nothing else, and it is a desperate struggle to will to go out beyond my limits.

The work *Training in Christianity* has great personal significance for me—does it follow that I should publish it right away? Perhaps I am one of the few who need such strong remedies—and should I then, instead of benefiting from it and myself beginning in real earnestness to become a Christian, should I first publish it? Fantastic!

The work and other works are ready; perhaps the time may come when it is suitable and I have the strength to do it and when it is truth in me.

In many ways it is true that the entire experience of writing is my upbringing or education—well, does that mean that instead of being in earnest about becoming a true Christian I am to become a phenomenon in the world?

CONSEQUENTLY *The Sickness unto Death* appears at this time, but pseudonymously and with me as editor. It is said to be "for upbuilding or edification." This category, edifying, is more than my category: poet.

Just as the Guadalquivir River (this occurred to me earlier and is somewhere in the journal [i.e., X^1 A 422]) plunges down somewhere into the earth, so is there also a stretch, the edifying, which carries my name. There is something (the esthetic) which is lower and is pseudonymous and something which is higher and is also pseudonymous, because as a person I do not correspond to it.

The pseudonymn is Johannes Anticlimacus in contrast to Climacus, who said he was not a Christian. Anticlimacus is the opposite extreme: a Christian on an extraordinary level—but I myself manage to be only a very simple Christian.

Training in Christianity can be published in the same way, but there is no hurry.

But nothing about my personality as a writer; it is false to want to anticipate during one's lifetime—this merely converts a person into the interesting.

On the whole, I must now venture in quite different directions. I must dare to believe that through Christ I can be saved from the power of melancholy in which I have lived; and I must try to be more economical.

X^1 A 510   n.d., 1849

Training in Christianity will be the last to be published. There I shall end for now.

Consequently the year '48 will be included, since the things by Anti-Climacus[26] are all from '48. The remainder is from '49. According to decision current writing will be shelved.

If *Training in Christianity* is published, what has been intimated many places elsewhere will be carried out—in all earnestness to set forth the possibility of offense. This is also related essentially to my task, which is continually to screw up the price by bringing a dialectic to bear. But for this reason, too, a pseudonym must be used. That which represents the dialectical element has always been under a pseudonym. To want to make it my own would be both untrue and an all too frightful and violent means of awakening.

x¹ A 615   n.d., 1849

As soon as the category "the single individual" goes out, Christianity is abolished. Then the individual will relate to God through the race, through an abstraction, through a third party—and then Christianity is *eo ipso* abolished. If this happens, then the God-man is a phantom instead of an actual prototype.

Alas, when I look at my own life! How infrequent the man who is so endowed for the life of the spirit and above all so rigorously schooled with the help of spiritual suffering—yet in the eyes of all my contemporaries I am fighting almost like a Don Quixote—it never occurs to them that it is Christianity; indeed, they are convinced of just the opposite.

Christendom as it is now makes Christ into a complete phantom as far as existence is concerned—although men do profess that Christ was a particular human being. They have no courage to believe existentially in the ideal.

Yes, it is true, the human race has grown away from Christianity! Alas, yes, in quite the same sense as a man grows away from ideals. For the young person the ideal is the ideal, but he relates to it with pathos. For the older person, who has grown away from the ideal, the ideal has become something quixotic and visionary, something which does not belong in the world of actuality.

In the hour of my death I shall repeat again and again, if possible, what every word in my writings testifies to: Never, never, with a single word have I given occasion for the mistaken notion that I personally mistook myself for the ideal—but I have been convinced that my striving has served to illuminate what Christianity is.

Reason and reflection have taken the ideal away from men, from Christendom, and have made it into something quixotic and visionary—consequently, being a Christian must be set a whole reflection farther back, being a Christian now comes to mean loving or desiring deeply to be a Christian, striving to be one: so enormous has the ideal now become.

In reference to this see the essay, *Armed Neutrality*, where I have paralleled this with the transition from being called σοφοι to being called φιλοσοφοι.

x¹ A 646   n.d., 1849

My Position in Regard to What Will Become the Situation in the Near Future

Presumably the Church is to be reformed now; synods are supposed to be held, there is to be balloting etc.

Even the strictest orthodox, even Rudelbach,[27] seem to want to take the position of relating themselves directly to all this and to do everything to make it as orthodox as possible.

I have always carried out flank attacks, wounding from behind.

At the very time that our most important task is supposed to be to reform the Church, I come with a contribution which screws up the price of being a Christian so high that it is doubtful that in the most rigorous sense there is a single true Christian living.

This is troublesome! Undeniably! But it is also sad and ridiculous that there is no awareness of what constitutes the basic corruption.

My continual task has been that of delaying—it is something like tapping a man on the shoulder when he is ready to jump and saying to him: May I have a word with you?

Right here is my point of coincidence with Mynster. This is the genuinely diverting means. But the fact is that in a certain sense Mynster is afraid of such a diverting means, especially when it is my hand. He himself has used it a little, but as a prudent official— here it is used by one who is nothing (one of those dangerous, suspicious people) and is used with absolute teleology.

Yet it may well turn out that Mynster is not the victim, if he will only be circumspect, keep quiet, and act calmly. I have always given my activity a turn as if I were a complete subordinate who operates seemingly under Mynster's supreme auspices and have given the impression that he nods his supreme approval and that this is decisive.

In a certain sense there is an uneasiness in this lest there occur, so to speak, a blink of the eye, a touch of uncertainty in the face.

My task quite rightly is entirely dialectical, and I cannot get away from the thought that I ought not get into a struggle with one who reminds me of my father.

x^1 A 660   n.d., 1849

In margin: Rudelbach on the Church constitution, par. cxxxi, pp. 243 etc.

This book has the merit of having shown that the state-Church gave rise to or contributed to giving rise to the proletariat.

How much there is to this Rudelbach seems not to have perceived.

In Christendom life is completely unchristian also in terms of what it means to live together with the common man and what this involves.

In this respect my life is like a discovery—alas, in a certain sense I can say that it is a dearly purchased discovery. It is unchristian and wicked to base the state on a substructure of men who are totally ignored and excluded from personal association—even though on Sunday there are touching sermons about loving "one's neighbor."

x^1 A 669   n.d., 1849

For the Postscript to The Accounting[28]

And now only one more thing, in order to be as truthful as possible. I know very well that there is a much more decisive Christian presentation of the essentially Christian, which, if I were the interpreter who corresponded to it, would lead me out beyond the established order. This I know very well, because for my own sake I have prepared such a presentation, written and in final copy.

But I have not wanted to communicate this presentation—for one thing I do not feel either strong enough or perfect enough in the truth or, above all, holy and pure enough to be the communicator. Secondly, because I have not dared take the responsibility of communicating something of this kind in our times, when philosophers, intellectuals, and the like would promptly make capital of the presentation for the interesting, the profound, the speculative in it. To be specific, however true such a communication is, if it does not have a correspondingly true communicator in whom it is the truth, who by his purity of life, by his sacrifices, yes, by his suffering and death, gives the cause true earnestness, then every such communication is only a contribution toward getting Christianity demonically taken in vain, since the Christian rule for Christian communication is that to present Christianity more decisively than my own life expresses it is forbidden as ungodliness. Finally, I have not wanted to communicate it, because I have not dared take upon myself the responsibility for perhaps bringing various weak persons almost to despair. I do not boast of humanitarianism in this, an idea which could occur only to people who have no conception at all of Christianity. Rather, I confess that it is a weakness on my part and a lack of genuine Christian love, which humanly speaking is and was and always will be a kind of cruelty. In view of what to my mind is the shocking brashness with which philosophers, intellectuals, the cultured, and the like have been busily occupied in going beyond Christianity, I have considered most earnestly whether it is not also my religious duty to go further, whether it is not God's will for me that I venture to present Christianity in its most decisive and true form, personally sinking under the weight of it but also preparing the equally certain doom of all those fools and bringing about an awakening, which could be to some purpose. In times of peace the world dozed off to sleep and came under the spell of delusions and illusions—under such circumstances it could well have been necessary. Then came the year '48. An awakening will come, I am sure, and therefore I have considered, since it was ambiguous to me anyway, whether I dared take the responsibility of calmly following my original reckoning, for from now on it will be of particular importance to strengthen the established order. Yet I confess that I understand very well that this could also be the moment [*Øieblikket*] to present Christianity most decisively, a moment which is almost like the moment when Christianity entered the world, that right now, when the attention of men is turned so exclusively to earthly, political, and national matters (just about as in Christ's time), is the moment to provide the contrast and by means of the contrast create an absolutely decisive tension, right now is the time to bring to mind Christ's words: My kingdom is not of this world. But I confess that I do not have the strength for this; I have not dared take the responsibility upon myself.

x⁵ b 205   n.d., 1849

Note. Recently a new pseudonym appeared: Anti-Climacus.[29] But this simply implies a stop; this is how one goes about dialectically effecting a stop: one points to something higher which examines a person critically and forces him back within his boundaries. October '49

The note which accompanies the final draft in the mahogany chest reads something like this.

x⁵ b 206   October, 1849

As the prototype [*Forbilledet*], Christ gives absolute expression to that which naturally no human being achieves: absolutely holding to God in all things. Consequently his life must with unqualified necessity collide absolutely with the world, with men, and he becomes the most forsaken and hated and wretched of all. Then the voice of mockery sounds: "He sticks to God—now let's see whether God wants him!"[30] The malice in this mockery is not anything peculiar to those Jews; it is in every man. For there is strife between man and God, and one must choose sides.

A man can experience something similar in a lesser degree. To be just moderately earnest about holding to God is the sure way to make a failure of everything temporal and earthly, for the more one holds to God the more he endeavors to make his cause pure and unselfish and his striving sacrificial—all of which becomes his misfortune; but the person who stakes his lot with men knows that the trick is to secure for himself earthly advantages which he can share with others.

Nevertheless men do notice that in spite of everything such a man's life is still a power, and they do not like him but almost hate him. And when finally there comes a sort of analogy to the suffering of Christ—being forsaken by God—the mockery rejoices and adores Nemesis for what happens to him. It sounds something like this: He should have stuck with us. Earlier it went like this: Join up with us, for to love us is to love God; to stick together with us is making the most of life.

Everyone who is just moderately earnest about holding to God is in a certain sense *eo ipso* squandered, even though for faith this is the most blessed of all. He misses everything in this life and is hated for it; if the latter happens, besides being squandered he is also sacrificed.

So it is; yet this must never be heard; if someone merely says this, his fate will be like that of one so squandered and sacrificed. It must not be heard, for it disturbs men's selfish doctrine that to stick together is to love God.

X^2 A 317   n.d., 1849

Appendix
A Word Concerning Myself

. . . . . If, however, someone were to say to me, "You who now for some time have lived and are living surrounded every day by the gossip, grinning, and stupidity of all these thousands—it seems to me there is something affected in your silence, in your never mentioning such things, or there is something affected in the serenity with which you speak of yourself, as if you were untouched by all this"—to him I would answer this way.

In the first place, when I am speaking (for the pseudonym de-

ceives), there is a very exalted person who listens—incidentally, this
is the case for every man, but most men perhaps do not think of it
—there is a very exalted person who is listening: God in heaven.
There in heaven he listens to what every man says. This I keep in
mind. No wonder, then, that my speech is not without a certain
solemnity. Moreover, I speak not with those thousands but with the
single individual before God—thus what is more remarkable is that
I do not speak ever so much more solemnly.

In margin: In the first place, bear in mind—something every
person ought to bear in mind concerning himself—bear in mind
that there is a very exalted person who is listening, God in heaven.
This I keep in mind. No wonder, then, that my speech is not without a certain solemnity. Moreover, I speak not with those thousands, but with the single individual before God—thus what is
more remarkable is that I do not speak ever so much more solemnly.

In the second place, I was told even as a small child, and as
solemnly as possible, that *they* spat upon Christ, even though he
was the truth, that *the crowd* ("those who went by") spat upon him
and said, "Fie upon you"—and he was the truth! This I have con-
cealed deep within my heart, and in order to conceal it all the
better I have even hidden my concealment of this thought in the
depths of my soul under the most contradictory appearances, for
I feared that it might slip out too soon, that I might be tricked out
of it and become a blank cartridge. This thought—which also
helped me understand readily and easily that simple wise man who
occupied me very much in my youth, *the intellectual martyr* whom
"numbers," "the crowd," persecuted and condemned to death—this
thought is my life, whose task until now has been chiefly an intellectual task, for which the struggle has been carried on religiously.
This thought is my life, which religiously struggles for the intellectual and the religious. I know with the greatest possible definiteness that I am on the right path—the encompassing gossip, grinning,
and stupidity of "the crowd" indicate that. No wonder then that
my speech is not without a certain solemnity and serenity, for the

path is the right one and I am on the right path, even though far behind.

If it is assumed that those who, after having voluntarily suffered for a long time the rudeness, mistreatment, and persecution of "the crowd" of contemporaries (consequently after being salted, as it were, "for every sacrifice ought to be salted")[31] and after having been mocked and spat upon by the crowd (consequently after having received the final consecration in advance), end by being crucified or beheaded or burned or broken on the wheel are in the first class in the essentially Christian order of ranking—if this is assumed (and, indeed, it is indisputable!), without saying too much about myself, I believe that I am about the lowest in the lowest, in class eight. No doubt I shall get no higher. But what a teacher once wrote about a pupil fits my life—the only difference is that he was not writing about me—"He retrogresses not without considerable industry." No doubt this was an unfortunate comment on the part of the teacher. Such a judgment can be regarded as advisable only in a special situation such as my own life. Yet the phrase "not without considerable industry" perhaps says too little, for I take great pains, am very industrious and hard-working, and it is also clear that the more pains I take the more I retrogress: thus with much industry I really do go backward more and more.

It is in this way that I hope to enter into eternity. Philosophically, how would it be possible to enter into eternity except by going backward, and from a Christian point of view, how would it be possible for me to enter into eternity without having more and more reverses? After first wanting to have him proclaimed king, did they not end by spitting upon Christ, who was the truth—and if I forgot everything, I would never forget, just as I have not yet forgotten, that this was told to me as a child and what an impression this made upon the child. It happens sometimes that a child still in the crib is engaged or pledged [forloves] to the one who is to become his wife or her husband. Religiously understood, even as a child I was pre-pledged [for-lovet]. Alas, I have paid dearly for having misunderstood life at one time and for having forgotten

—that I was pledged! On the other hand I have also once in my life experienced the most beautiful and blessed, to me so indescribably satisfying, gratification, because in the step which I took at that time, in the danger to which I *voluntarily* exposed myself, I understood perfectly that I was pre-pledged and was perfectly reconciled to it. Engaged, pledged to the love which from the beginning and up to this moment, in spite of my many sins and errors, has encompassed me—of whom it truly can be said that he sinned much, but of whom it nevertheless perhaps is not wholly untrue to say that he loved much—encompassed me with a love which infinitely surpasses my understanding, with a fatherly love "in comparison with which even the most loving father[32] is but a stepfather."

Just one thing more, something which I emphasize with all the intensity and earnestness of one making a deathbed wish—when I compare myself to those glorious ones in the various classes in the essentially Christian order of ranking (in which I am as far as possible from the first class, in the lowest of the lowest, in class eight), I no doubt have a certain tragic advantage, yet still in one sense a real advantage, over them. It seems to me that if a person is personally pure or even approximately pure, perfect, and holy, the world's opposition to the truth must grieve him to the extent that he would soon die of grief. But I am no saint; I am a penitent, for whom suffering can be very beneficial, and for whom, precisely as a penitent, it is personally satisfying to suffer. Yes, if I were contemporary with a purer spirit, it would gratify me to shift, if possible, all the crowd's mockery and mistreatment from him to myself. As far as having to endure mistreatment is concerned, I believe it is a superior advantage that I, who have the honor of serving the truth, by being personally a penitent (for past and present wrongdoings) such as this (but only such as this), meet the mistreatment by men at the right place when it is turned against me, who have no doubt brought off the deception with extraordinary success, the deception (which to a degree is possibly an invention of melancholy) of being regarded as the most frivolous of all.

X[5] B 153   n.d., 1849

Addition to "The Accounting"[33]

The fact that I here speak *directly* about myself may be called, I know, an *inconsistency*—that is, insofar as anyone has gotten the notion that I am pure idea; on the contrary, it is entirely consistent with what I have always said about myself, that I am a poor solitary individual; and there is a *consistency* in that it was not at all vain desire or egotism or eccentricity which made me decide to be silent. My situation is this: suffering under the obligation to understand myself—or in any case believing I had to understand myself as a more unhappy exception in one respect, I have applied all my spiritual and mental powers and devoutly dedicated them (encouraged also by external circumstances) properly to become *aware*, if possible, of ideality and to be able to make others *aware* of it. I am incapable of more, I demand no more; I thank Providence unceasingly that this has been granted me, indescribably more than I had expected. But, after reflecting so much and so intensely all these years on "the single individual," I am far from concluding that it was a mistake, a misunderstanding. No, I have come to the conclusion that this thought is the thought of eternal truth, but if it is to be carried through on the greatest possible scale, no man is able to endure it, let alone for a whole lifetime, even less if he is denied the advantage of being freed of financial worries. The truth in an individual is the purest spiritual power, but it means also to renounce and unconditionally to miss everything earthly and temporal on a scale appropriate to being pure spirit. On the other hand, to the same degree as the numerical is advanced in relation to truth, to the same degree physical power is mistaken for spiritual power; but since man as man is not pure spirit, he needs community as well as earthly and temporal means. This is, if you will, a tragic truth, but even if this is to be conceded, it does not follow that one goes so far as to make the numerical determine what is truth and to regard this matter of "the single individual" as falsehood and fantasy, instead of making an admission concerning himself, that it is the truth which is too high for him, and then humbling himself under it, so that he maintains a relationship to it partly through the admission and partly through a striving, weak and imperfect though it be.

$$x^5 \text{ B } 255 \quad \text{n.d., } 1849\text{-}50$$

In some cases protracted reflection about willing or not willing in relation to a very decisive step is not simply to be explained as a lack of character. On the contrary, this continued reflection may be a necessary attrition which is the very condition for really acting decisively. . . .

$$x^2 \text{ A } 636 \quad \text{n.d., } 1850$$

The Requirement—Indulgence

The requirement is the universal, that which holds good for all, the criterion by which everyone must be measured. Therefore the requirement is what must be proclaimed. The teacher has to declare the requirement and in this way incite unrest. He dare not scale down the requirement.

Indulgence must not be proclaimed. Indeed, it cannot be proclaimed, since it is completely different for different people in their innermost private understanding with God.

The proclamation of the requirement is to drive men to God and Christ in order to find what indulgence they need, what indulgence they dare ask for before God, and the proclamation of the requirement constantly holds them to God.

But we have turned the relationship around. The teacher (pastor and priest) does not proclaim the requirement but indulgence. Instead of acknowledging that the indulgence is the deepest secret of the individual conscience with God, face to face with the requirement, we have turned the relationship around and for mutual contentment and edification declare indulgence pure and simple. The requirement is omitted completely or we say it pertained only to the apostles and then each one enthusiastically declares indulgence to the others—indulgence, which is still one of the prerogatives of God's majesty and thus can be bestowed only by him to the single individual, that is, to every individual but to each one separately.

Do I have the right to say to another person (except in the very special situation of anxiety and illness etc., although I still would have to say to him that he must turn to God and there he will find peace): God does not require this of you (even though it is the New Testament requirement), not to mention whether I have the right to take it upon myself to be a teacher, to be paid for it, and then to proclaim to an entire congregation: God does not require this (even though it is the New Testament requirement), God is gracious etc.?—No, this I have no right to do. I must proclaim the requirement, and then I must add: If it is too burdensome for you, turn to God (as I myself, who also need indulgence, have done); then you will surely come to an understanding with him, but also before him, about what can be conceded to you.

But we have taken indulgence in vain. It has become a kind of fable which we tell to one another (this is something like "preaching"), that God is not very strict etc. And yet the intention is quite different.

God is the sole bestower of grace. He wants every person (educated up to it through proclamation of the requirement) to turn, each one separately, to him and to receive, each one separately, the indulgence which can be granted to him. But we men have turned the relationship around, robbed or tricked God out of the royal prerogative of grace and then put out a counterfeit grace.

X³ A 72   n.d., 1850

Another Dimension to Being a Christian

What is called humanity today is not purely and simply humanity but a diffused form of the essentially Christian.

Originally the procedure was this: with "the universally human consciousness" as the point of departure, to accept the essentially Christian.[34] Now the procedure is this: from a point of origin which already is a diffused form of the essentially Christian, to become Christian.

Ergo, there is another dimension to being a Christian.

Here, as I have developed in *Armed Neutrality*, it is apparent that the procedure turns out to be one of instituting reflection on a full level, deeper and more inward, something like the change from σοφοι to φιλοσοφοι, simply because the task has become enormously greater.

x³ A 204   n.d., 1850

Christianity—Suffering

In respect to everything else in the world, it holds that if I begin something, it is possible that I may succeed but it is also possible that I may fail—but not in respect to Christianity. Here if suffering does not come, then my life has not expressed true Christianity at all.

If this is not true, then the prototype [*Forbilledet*] is in some way an untruth. Either the prototype expressed something merely accidental (that by living at a certain time he met with opposition etc.) and therefore is not essentially the prototype, or there ought to be more prototypes (one expressing that the truth is to suffer, another that it is to float, etc.) and in this case "the prototype" is indeed untrue, for it means only one.

But you say: "If a man is a professing Christian and then otherwise lives as the others, he must leave his fate in the world to God."

I am not going to speak now about the potential precariousness of professing Christ if nothing more is meant by it than is now understood in Christendom—being baptized as a child, etc., or as a theological candidate seeking a position—for if this is professing Christ, then the chances are that there will be no collision with the world; whereas from a Christian viewpoint one certainly takes upon himself great responsibility by participating in such deceptions. But I will not speak of this. But in addition to professing Christ (saying I am a Christian and believing what a Christian is required to believe), acting in an essentially Christian manner is also required (which corresponds in particular to the presence of a "prototype" and true Christianity as imitation [*Efterfølgelse*]).

Try it, then, enact in your life an action marked by Christian quality, and you will see collision for sure. This world lies in sheer relativity—and the Christian quality is absolute—such action must in life and in death collide with actuality [*Virkeligheden*]. Certainly no human being, not even an apostle, can bear the absolute when he enacts it, so that to bear it is to be it—which also accounts for everything breaking, the veil of the temple, the graves, all existence [*Tilværelsen*], all this relativity—but in addition, the collision will endanger his life.

But the situation is that action characterized essentially by Christian quality is perhaps not seen once in each generation; it reaches only a certain degree, and then comes the collision.

x³ A 283   n.d., 1850

Indirect Communication

It is not true that direct communication is superior to indirect communication. No, no. But the fact is that no man has ever been born who could use the indirect method even fairly well, to say nothing of using it all his life. For we human beings need each other, and in that there is already a directness.

Only the God-man is in every respect indirect communication from first to last. He did not need men, but they infinitely needed him; he loves men, but according to his conception of what love is; therefore he does not change in the slightest toward their conception, does not speak directly in such a way that he also surrenders the possibility of offense—which his existence [*Existents*] in the guise of servant is.

When a person uses the indirect method, there is in one way or another something demonic—but not necessarily in the bad sense —about it, as, for example, with Socrates.

Direct communication indeed makes life far easier. On the other hand, the use of direct communication may be humiliating for a person who has used indirect communication perhaps selfishly (therefore demonically in a bad sense).

I have frequently felt impelled to use direct communication (it must be remembered, of course, that even when I did, it was far from being carried through completely and, indeed, it was only for a short time), but it seemed to me as if I wanted to be lenient with myself and that I could achieve more by holding out. Whether there is pride here as well, God knows best—before God I dare neither affirm nor deny this, for who knows himself well enough for this?

When I look back on my life, I must say that it seems to me not impossible that something higher hid behind me. It was not impossible. I do not say more. What have I done, then? I have said: For the present I use no means which would disturb this possibility, for example, by *premature* direct communication. The situation is like that of a fisherman when he sees the float move—maybe it means a strike, maybe it is due to the motion of the water. But the fisherman says: I will not pull up the line; if I do, I indicate that I have surrendered this possibility; perhaps it will happen again and prove to be a bite.

For me indirect communication has been as if instinctive within me, because in being an author I no doubt have also developed myself, and consequently the whole movement is backwards, which is why from the very first I could not state my plan directly, although I certainly was aware that a lot was fermenting within me. Furthermore, consideration for "her" required me to be careful. I could well have said right away: I am a religious author. But later how would I have dared to create the illusion that I was a scoundrel in order if possible to help her. Actually it was she—that is, my relationship to her—who taught me the indirect method. She could be helped only by an untruth about me; otherwise I believe she would have lost her mind. That the collision was a religious one would have completely deranged her, and therefore I have had to be so infinitely careful. And not until she became engaged again and married did I regard myself as somewhat free in this respect.

Thus through something purely personal I have been assisted to something on a far greater scale, something I have gradually come to understand more and more deeply.

x^3 A 413   n.d., 1850

ENTRIES PERTAINING TO
AN OPEN LETTER

Dr. Rudelbach and I

We shall never understand one another.

For him it has long since been definitely settled that he is a Christian. And now he busies himself with history and the external forms of the Church. He has never felt the disquietude of the idea, wondering every single day whether he is now a Christian or not. "Never"—no, because one who has felt this once, one day, one hour, does not let go of it during his entire life, or it never lets go of him.

The idea has involved me in personal self-concern, and therefore I can never find time for projects, for I must begin every day with this concern: Are you a Christian now? Indeed, perhaps this very day there will be an existential collision which will make it clear that you are not a Christian at all.

x^4 A 20   n.d., 1851

On the draft cover, bluish-grey:
The article on Rudelbach
> A part which has not been used, but which may have some significance.

x^5 B 120   n.d., 1851

Notations on proofs of An Open Letter Prompted by a Reference to Me by Dr. Rudelbach *(S.V. XIII, pp. 436-44):*

4. ["the second half is false," p. 47 above] since I have never sought to use external means or proposed them or had anything

to do with something as great as "the Church" but have limited my activity to "the single individual."

6. ["that external conditions and forms will help," p. 50 above]. As I see it the so-called old-time Christians* are therefore at this time in the process of plunging full blast, jubilating** in song and dance, besides, toward what (Christianly understood) is perhaps the most dangerous of all illusions.

X^5 B 121   n.d., 1851

* who have become, to be sure, terribly modern.
** "like a bird rushing into the snare."

Addition to X^5 B 121:

With just a few strokes on the chart of our situation let me sketch the movements of my operation.

In my opinion we ordinary men may be content (and Christianly this is also permissible), may be humbly content with being Christians in quiet inwardness. When this is the case, one may also very well be satisfied with the given external forms—yes, it is precisely and truly Christian not to be occupied with external forms. However, I do believe that greater effort ought to be made to develop a competent clergy who would work for the inward deepening of Christianity in individuals* and to guarantee the commonwealth a sound cadre of plain, good Christians (who constitute an indispensable foundation) who are not occupied with reforming either state or Church.

* *In margin:* it would be desirable and it is necessary that the pastors strive in a higher degree for the inward deepening of Christianity in themselves and in individuals

If anyone believes he cannot be satisfied with being such a Christian in hidden inwardness but aspires to something higher, then, in my opinion, there is Christianly only one thing higher—martyrdom, in which one walks alone, forsaken by men and also, humanly speaking, forsaken by God. The frightful, narrow way of this martyrdom, its frightful splendor, must be stated and portrayed because Christians should never forget that it exists [*er til*], because if it is forgotten, the average Christian would become all too secular, but if it is remembered, being humbled under this lofty ideal will help develop inwardness in us ordinary Christians.

But there is still one thing more—the way of the lower level: sectarianism, partisanship, politicizing in the realm of the Church, reformation by way of balloting, etc. All this ought to be opposed. It is sad to see that the so-called old-time Christians—perhaps as a result of having once felt a pressure—now have broken loose all the more and join together with what in a Christian sense is their opposite, and now in their old age they represent a most impoverished Christianity (a composite of politics and Christianity); whereas in their earlier days and especially in the earliest times they represented the original, primitive old Christianity.

This is my opinion. The fault of this age is fancying itself to be an age of reformation and, curiously enough, wanting to reform *en masse*. But Providence sends no reformer. If it sends anything, it sends a servant or two—to reform the reformers.

"There is something antiquated about this." To be sure. But watch out. With the help of the year 1848 it will not be long before it will have become the newest of all.

X⁵ B 124   n.d., 1851

Addition to X⁵ B 121:

Conclusion

There is something curious about the whole thing; I am almost tempted to believe that Dr. [Rudelbach] has not read any of my writings at all but that it only seems so to him and that he then naturally also must be able to designate the significance of all these writings and to assign them a place in foreign literature and in our own. But I do not find this inexplicable at all. If someone, like me, has read only a few works, he is easily able to keep the lines straight. But if one has read an enormous mass of books, such a mistake can easily take place. It is like many other things. A person who has never travelled farther than Roskilde can easily and definitely know where he has been. A much travelled person, however, one who has travelled around the world many times and been all over, may very readily think and say, when some place is mentioned which he has not actually visited: Yes, I was there the summer of 1835; there is a very high tower with a magnificent view, etc. (but there is no tower at all). So it is also with the notion that the point of my work as an author is supposed to be emancipation of the Church from the state. Inasmuch as I am not occupied with the Church* I am even less occupied with its emancipation from the state—just as there can only be very figurative reference to a view from the tower if there is no tower.

In margin: but with influencing the single individual

x^5 B 125   n.d., 1851

Addition to x^5 B 121:

Filled with self-concern through having been wounded by the ideals but nevertheless ineffably happy because of this and grateful for it. For, if one is human, as far as the ideals are concerned it is the most fearful presumption that could arise in a human being to want to be more than an unhappy lover, however burning with zeal one's striving may be; but, if one has become the unhappy lover, to be able to forget for one moment that this is the greatest good fortune that can befall a man would be the most dreadful ingratitude, a proof that he no longer sees the ideals which indescribably move and captivate even the most unhappy of all their unhappy lovers—if he sees them.

x^5 B 126   n.d., 1851

The Old Orthodox

who claimed that they were the only true Christians in Denmark.

I have nothing against their separating from us—but it is indefensible that they should achieve this by balloting and without giving up the claim that they are the true Church.

But this is supposed to be the tactic—and then judgment is supposed to fall upon Mynster and his party.

In what frame of mind could the honest Spandet[35] make his proposal? Did he look upon it as similar to a motion about gas-street-lighting and the like—if so, then of course a vote may be taken, but it was certainly improper to make his proposal in this vein. Or if he insists that he has regarded it as a matter of conscience, how in the world can he then be satisfied with serving a matter of conscience (which as a "royal service" not only must be promoted quickly and be put through—but must be put through or the one commissioned falls)—by making a motion for balloting and then seeing how many votes it will get.

Even if it did go through, the cause would still be wrongly served, and an *indirect* proof would be given that it is not a matter of conscience for him and that he has bitten off too much.

And if it fails to pass, then perhaps he will step forth in character.

X⁴ A 36   n.d., 1851

The Old Orthodox would like to withdraw from the whole Church and yet reserve for themselves the status of being the true Church, and perhaps also (as Rudelbach seems to indicate in his book on the constitution of the Church),[36] keep all the Church property for themselves, which per capita is not so insignificant, since the Church property is rather considerable and, according to Rudelbach, the true Christians are very few.

X⁴ A 37   n.d., 1851

Dr. Rudelbach

is really vapid. Apparently he has not read the portion in *Training in Christianity* (stating that Christianity does not exist)[37] in such a way that it even remotely occurred to him to compare himself with the ideal and ask himself: But are you yourself a Christian? No, he is definitely and unalterably convinced that he and his party are Christians. And now he has been delighted with the statement and has had Mynster in mind.

And I, on the other hand, quite simply had only myself in mind.

x^4 A 46   n.d., 1851

That Christianity Always Involves a Double Danger

is shown even by my life's fragmentary approximation of a Christian existence.

The present step against Rudelbach[38] involves a double danger, for those who really gain by it leave me stuck with it—yes, ultimately they may even use it against me.

For the most part men beware of venturing out except when there is only one danger. So it is with Grundtvig at the moment, for if he were to introduce the concept of Christian freedom in a Christian way he would get the secular-minded against him as well as the ecclesiastical establishment. But he unchristianly removes the one danger by a coalition with the friends of the peasants.

x^4 A 79   n.d., 1851

The End of the Affair
by
S. Kierkegaard

In this paper [*The Fatherland*, Nos. 37, February 13, 1851, and 38, February 14, 1851], Dr. Rudelbach, by stating some points of difference, has now explained in somewhat more detail that we two do not agree.

Well, wasn't that just what I said? For how did the affair begin? Toward the end of the little book on civil marriage there is a passage in which Dr. R. succinctly states his whole point of view and his plan of operation: "What is rightly called routine- and state-Christianity must go. We must fight for the emancipation of the Church from the state by means of free institutions, one of which is civil marriage." This means that the goal is external change through the use of external means. The following note is added to this text: "This is exactly what Søren Kierkegaard seeks to impress upon, to imprint upon, and, as Luther says, to drive home to all those who will listen."

Consequently we two, Dr. R. and I, agree, completely agree! And I, knowing my task and my responsibility, I, who have guarded in the most anxious fear and trembling of conscience lest even a jot or tittle hinting at external change be mixed into these many books but with the most rigorous abstemiousness have fought alone, and solely with the weapons of the spirit, for the inward deepening of Christianity in the single individual, I regard the disagreement between Dr. R. and me to be comparable in kind and scope to that between two physicians (yet it must be kept in mind that in the Christian sense I do not pass myself off as a physician but am rather myself a patient), one of whom thought that external means should be used in a given situation (or at least the addition of external means) and the other thought that only internal remedies should be used, yes, that the use of external remedies amounted to a conspiracy with the disease, a greater danger than if nothing at all were done either with surgery or with drugs!—But enough of this; the works testify to this, and besides, in my earlier article I found and used the occasion to point this out quite adequately. And then we two agree, totally agree!

Thus I find myself prompted and obliged, especially in view of present circumstances,* to make a slight objection: that we two

---

* The present circumstances are such that every moment these fatal political encroachments are menacing the religious [*changed from*: churchly] domain. And such encroachments become doubly alarming when a mistaken orthodoxy

simply do not agree, that I have worked simply and solely for the
inward deepening of Christianity in the single individual, and that
for the rest (this was added after the article against Dr. R., which
was published over my name, had really ended), I humbly acknowledge that there is a far higher task, that a person may collide with
the established order in such a way that external change becomes
a matter of conscience, so that he must operate not only along the
lines of being a witness to the truth but with "the apostle" as the
prototype; yet if a person must or desires to venture out in this way,
his operation cannot possibly be fashioned with balloting as the
model and he cannot march to the tune of "Let's get together." In
fact, I made it [*changed from:* God knows I made this objection]
in a way that seems uncalled for, because, among other things,
Dr. R. had used a very appreciative statement about me, and then
it is always unpleasant to have to make an objection; with such a
point of departure it is very easy to infringe on a man. But, after
all, I have not had great returns as an author, and therefore I have
wanted at least the satisfaction that what I have intended should

---

or hyperorthodoxy (which supposedly would be absolutely opposed by its very
nature) perhaps inadvertently becomes the amicable ingredient so that political
radicalism and this pious radicalism come to stick together through voting by
ballot in a *bona caritate* almost like—yes, what I am about to say is *e concessis*
according to pious radicalism's own rigorous conception of the world and
secular-mindedness, for I have a milder conception—almost like Geert West-
phaler's unintentional drinking to an oath of friendship with the executioner.[39]
Under such circumstances no doubt even the most honest orthodox person—he
most likely of all—will admit that I have expressed myself both cautiously and
circumspectly when (not as Dr. R. reports, that I have summarily accused him
as guilty of this "confounded confusion of Christianity and politics"), sweeping
before my own door, I have said: Nothing alarms me as much as anything which
even remotely smacks of this confounded confusion of Christianity and politics.
And no doubt such a person will also agree with me that Dr. R. does not report
quite accurately when he says that I "reject" all free associations as a whole.
I have not altogether rejected anything; I have said that I have a suspicion
about the kind of associations in which one in formal unity sticks together
with his qualitative opposite, which is being all too free-and-easy in freely
associating.

stand as clearly as possible. And in this respect that little note was extremely misleading.

Therefore I make the objection that we two do not agree. And this is what Dr. R. has followed up in a freer discourse which sticks neither to the text nor to the note nor to the matter itself: the text and the note. Dr. R. presents a few points of difference: we two do not agree.

But what about that note? And how can Dr. R. possibly begin his article by saying that I have seriously misunderstood him? I was the one who stated immediately that we two disagree, that there must be a misunderstanding on Dr. R.'s part. The affair between Dr. R. and me is not a discussion concerning Christianity and politics beginning with my open letter but is that little note in which R. summarily maintained that we two agree. It was not I who began, not I who *invited* discussion; on the contrary, it was that little note by R., and it was I who in a newspaper article *defended* myself against what the note seemed to intend: that without further ado I ought to be regarded as one who is in complete agreement with Dr. R. Therefore my signature stood about midway in the article, indicating that the affair with Dr. R. had really terminated.

But now the disagreement has certainly been substantiated. To me this is the main point. If. Dr. R. wants to say that this is a misunderstanding—with pleasure! This is of no importance to me. On the other hand, it is of importance to me that it be clearly maintained that we two disagree. "But, honored friend, this is a misunderstanding." Yes, yes, then let it be a misunderstanding.

One can hardly be more compliant, and Dr. R. cannot possibly demand more, especially in a case in which the disagreement, according to my conception, is so manifest that I pledge myself to make it comprehensible to a child, although my reader may well smile at my situation, he who easily sees with half an eye what I could—if not see—at least know without trying. And now since everything, after all, is supposed to be free in our time, since we are to have civil marriage without wedding ceremony and union, so I too shall be free, and I hope that no one joins me together with Dr. R. by forced union if I have even the slightest misgiving about it.

The disagreement, therefore, has now been substantiated.

I see, however, and with joy, that there is something else which has remained unchanged; I see it with joy, partly because, as mentioned, I know Dr. R. from my father's house, partly because Dr. R. is our learned and expert Dr. R., and finally because it is after I have had to write an article such as my first one—I see with joy that Dr. R. has maintained unchanged his friendly good-will toward me. Yes, this time it seems to have found an even stronger expression than the first time, when toward the end of the article it is said of me that I have made the one great sacrifice the world does not know—my time, my diligence, my life.

* *

I find this last portion very fine, very fine of Dr. R.; I urgently request him to accept my thanks for it.

But it would not be fine of me to keep silent about it, for what is said of me there is much too much. I still am *essentially* only a poet. I have had the task of laying emphasis upon ideality, of applying the ideals, but then the additional task of seeing to it, for the sake of God in heaven, that the horrible thing does not happen that I am confused with the perfection which I portray. But with respect to my undertaking, I have not sacrificed either my time or my labor, and least of all my life. The most that can truthfully be said of me is that I, in the service of the idea, have dedicated or consecrated my time, my labor, during part of my life, for the fact that I have worked gratis can signify at most that I have sacrificed some money and signifies least of all what I have done least of all—sacrificed my life. On the contrary, to describe my seven years of activity as an author I may use the words of the poet: *Ich habe gelebt und geliebt.* I have lived, lived much in a few years, and I have loved—yes . . . . . yes, the ideals, yes, indescribably, and in all honesty I still do. I have not been cheated out of this love, and it has not been pounded out of me either, but has only been made more intense. Yet I am only a poet. I have been permitted to go on living in almost the childlike situation of a father's son, occupied. early and late in portraying the ideals and in testifying that such glorious ones have lived, who, by stepping forth in character, have shown that they had a cause of conscience or that they still were related ethically to the idea and therefore neither sought first of all to become a crowd nor babbled nonsense about being a crowd, hopefully anticipating the results of balloting—such glorious ones of whom it is literally true that they have sacrificed—for we can all, the clergy as well as the layman, talk, sing, orate, and talk big about sacrificing—but sacrificed!—note this well—sacrificed! O, this is so elevated: they have *sacrificed*, sacrificed time and labor (and in return they received nothing but the ingratitude of all!), honor and property (and the reward, the only reward, but all the more abundant, was mockery), a cozy life lived in harmony with men, friendship and love and life, and all for the sake of truth! I, on the other hand, am essentially only a poet who happens also to have been wronged. From the very beginning and continually I have been accused of being a colossal egotist. Perhaps they still do not understand me, that my sickness may be just the opposite. Through much association with the ideals in quiet solitariness I have learned to hate myself, learned to understand what a wretched bungler I am; many a time I have felt that my life could be bought for four shillings—to such a degree have I learned to hate myself. But I love —yes . . . . . yes, the ideals, yes, indescribably!

Added in margin: as one who loves what wounds: the ideals, what infinitely detains: the ideals, as one who loves what, humanly speaking, makes a man unhappy: the ideals, what teaches "to flee to grace": the ideals, what in a higher sense makes a man inde-scribably happy, the ideals—if in the self-concern of the infinite he can learn properly to hate himself. Indescribably happy, although he nevertheless has had to and has to admit humbly to himself that there is something infinitely higher which he has not reached, and on the other hand so indescribably happy that he simply does not feel it to be something lacking if he perhaps does not happen to find time either to dance or to vote or to clink glasses.[40]

x^5 B 128   n.d., 1851

For "The Accounting."[41] Something, however, which is not to be included.

Concerning Myself

Inasmuch as before God I regard my entire work as an author as my own upbringing or education, I could say: But I have remained silent so long lest, in relation to what I understand before God to be my own education, by speaking prematurely I become guilty of talking out of school. This could then be added to the passage in the final draft of "The Accounting": Before God I call this my upbringing or education etc.

I would have liked very much to use this very expression; lyrically it would have gratified me to use this expression. But there is something else that holds me back. As is frequently the case, the most humble expression seen from another angle is the very one that is apt to say too much, and so it is here. Precisely this humble expression would accentuate the fact that it is my education, almost in the sense of my being an authority. It is simpler as it stands in "The Accounting," with the addition that I need further education, and the tone is such that it can be said of every man.

x^4 A 85   n.d., 1851

My Tactic—

always *disputere* only *e concessis* (to take a man's words when he says something great about himself and then to press the existential consequences upon him), might seem to be "villainous malice and envy." By no means, it is admiration. But it is the admiration of reflection which looks where it is going, and ethically it is irony, which the lack of character in our age needs.

x^4 A 101   n.d., 1851

. . . . . cannot be formed according to the paradigm of balloting (balloting, balloting with discussion, balloting without discussion— O balloting, from, in, with, upon, by balloting) or be done according to the popular song: Let's a few of us get together, hurrah, hurrah, hurrah. Street-lighting and clothes and, with all due respect, the sanitation department can be reformed in this manner; but let us be men: Christianity does not lend itself to reformation in this way.

x^4 A 102   n.d., 1851

. . . . . You have 1,000 pastors—if you had only one who had nevertheless a little to sacrifice for the sake of Christianity, you would be better served. You want to reform the Church—then get first of all one Christian, and let him reform the Church.

x^4 A 117   n.d., 1851

My Sights

are always directed toward this: Christianity actually does not exist, that is to say, existentially, and this is also why I call myself a poet.

For the sake of this aim it is naturally of importance to me to exclude anything which could be misleading in this respect. At one time it was believed that the need was for a speculative system— this was misleading, for then it was tacitly conceded that we are Christians, that this was certain and that everything was all right, since the need was only for a system. Nowadays people want to reform the Church—this is equally misleading, as if everything were all right with all of us as Christians. Here, you see, is the difference between me and Rudelbach, who speaks only of a little party which he calls the Church—they are the true Christians, which, however, I do not think is so.

x^4 A 118   n.d., 1851

Amazing!

Once the objection against Christianity (and this was right at the time when it was most evident what Christianity is) was that it was unpatriotic, a danger to the state, revolutionary—and now Christianity has become patriotism and a state-Church.

Once the objection against Christianity (and this was right at the time when it was most evident what Christianity is and the objection was made by the genuinely keen-eyed pagans) was that it was anti-human—and now Christianity has become humanity.

Once Christianity was an offense to the Jews and foolishness to the Greeks, and now it is—culture. For Bishop Mynster the mark of true Christianity is culture.

And now if Dr. Rudelbach will give up his office and step forth as a solitary man, get rid of misconceived collaboration in the form of political favor, and declare that he is no Christian and that Christianity does not exist at all—that would be something. But this whole muddle of voting by every Tom, Dick, and Harry, which allows for a host of illusions—no, this is nonsense.

x⁴ A 126   n.d., 1851

Vinet

March 9

I have now obtained *Der Sozialismus in seinem Principe betrachtet* [*Socialism Considered According to Its Principles*] by Vinet, translated by Hofmeister.

Reading his foreword to the little book has been enough.

He is not the man [the awaited existential ethicist]. He is a brilliant author who writes something about the single individual but is not in character, does not operate in character, is not existentially higher than all discussion—no, no, he writes something which he then submits to public opinion; he palavers with the public in the usual author fashion.

But nevertheless there is spirit.

x⁴ A 185   March 9, 1851

Addition to x⁴ A 185 *in margin:*

It was Vinet for whom Rudelbach shouted in his book on civil marriage, saying that Vinet and I are in agreement. Curiously enough, I then requested a book by him from the University Library. It was on loan. Some time later it was sent to me. A few days later the librarian told me that the one who had had the book would like to have it again. I returned it at once. It turned out that Martensen was the one who had had it. It was a large book by Vinet in French and for that reason I did not read any of it. But today I myself have obtained the little book which I had ordered.

X⁴ A 186   March 9, 1851

Independence

How is it that in our time only a wealthy person is regarded as an independent man? I wonder if it is not because we have completely forgotten or transformed into a fable the fact that being able to live on roots, water, and bread is a more secure independence.

X⁴ A 257   n.d., 1851

Conversation with Bishop Mynster, May 2

As I entered I said that this was just about the time he usually travelled on his visitations and I usually liked to call upon him some time before.

So we talked together about the minister and the department, which I do not note down since it does not concern my cause.

Then the conversation was drawn to more recent events. I mentioned again the tactic with my latest pseudonym[42] and pointed out how without it I could not have taken the position against Rudelbach, which he admitted. I then repeated that even if he had something against this book of mine, which was possible, it was nevertheless a defense of the established order.

Then I turned suddenly to his book[43] and said outright that I had not come to thank him for my copy because there was something in it which I could not approve, and this was why I had been delinquent about visiting him.

We talked about this; yet he was momentarily startled when I turned the conversation this way. So we talked about this. He maintained essentially, as I could well understand, that he had merely said that Goldschmidt[44] was talented, whereupon I pointed out that this could be understood as an understatement. I reminded him that he, too, had enemies and how an enemy might construe his behavior. I repeated again and again that what concerned me was whether his reputation had not suffered too much by directing attention to Goldschmidt in this way.* I pointed out to him that he ought to have demanded a revocation by G.; I told him that with his permission I would show how he should have done it—that is, demanded a revocation. The precariousness of it all lay, I told him, in this, that he should keep in mind that he has to represent prestige—and that it was impossible for me to defend his conduct. I pointed out to him how he now had G. in his power, that he could give a turn to the affair—one usually brings out the good in a man by means of the good; the fact that M. had directed attention to G. in this way ought to have made G. aware that a revocation was necessary; since it was lacking, what had been done was also of a different character. But M. was of the opinion that there was still something in the fact that G. had remained silent. I explained again how insidious G. was and that it probably would appear some time.

Then I said to him: It may seem strange that youth speaks to age in this manner, but for the present will you permit me to do so and allow me to give you some advice: If there is anything about me of which you disapprove, if you would like to give me a whack, do it, do it; I can take it and shall see to it that you do not suffer for it; but above all do not do it in such a way that your own prestige comes to suffer thereby. It is your prestige that concerns me.

Again and again I repeated: "I want it said plainly and bluntly," "I want my conscience to be clear," "It must be noted that I have said that I cannot approve of it" (and as I said it, I bent over the table and wrote, as it were, with my hand). To this he replied: "Well, it is very explicit." And I saw to it that every time I said this he replied and indicated that he had heard it.

In other respects my conversation was permeated by all the affection for him I received from my father and still have. I talked much longer than usual. Incidentally, he was more friendly and attentive than usual today. I did something which I otherwise do not do—I spoke a little with him about his family, a subject he brought up himself by saying that his daughter was to be married. And I spoke a little with him about himself, about the joy of his old age, and how grateful he must be. And then again—that he must be sure to watch out for his prestige.

Usually he has to be pressed when I speak of paying him a visit, and generally he is in the habit of saying that I might better come some other time, without saying when. This he did not do today. On the contrary, he said that I would be welcome. And when I said: Is another time perhaps more convenient to you, he replied: Come at the specified time. To which I answered: I would certainly prefer to come at that time; it is very special to me; I am accustomed to it, and "tradition is still a great force." (This was an allusion to something in the conversation.)

And so it went—Thanks, good friend, etc.

I parted from him on the most friendly terms possible.

Incidentally, when we spoke together of Goldschmidt he made an attempt to point out that he had used "talented" for Goldschmidt and "gifted" for me and that the latter meant much more. To which I answered: That is of no consequence, the question here is your prestige. Thereupon he abandoned this attempt.**

On the whole I was happy to have spoken with him. My affection for him belongs to him, after all, and it does not help much to put in print how devoted to him I am—it would never be understood anyway.

x⁴ A 270 May 2, 1851

Addition to x⁴ A 270 *in margin:*
* He said that G. was a useful man and that one ought to utilize such people. I replied that there is an impatience which sees only what appears advantageous at the moment but which is dangerous,

and that it was a question of whether or not he had not bought too dearly by paying with his prestige.

x⁴ A 271   n.d., 1851

Addition to x⁴ A 270 *in margin:*
** The dubious aspect (of the extent to which Mynster was unwilling to affront me by grouping me with Goldschmidt in this way) was something which up until now I have not wanted to note down although I hid it in my memory. When I said that he at least ought to have let G. first disavow his past, M. answered: Then I would have to read through all of his numerous books. Thus I was supposed to believe that M. was actually ignorant of the fact that there was a paper called *The Corsair*, that G. had edited it for six years, and that M. did not understand that this was what I was aiming at!

x⁴ A 272   n.d., 1851

And this also took place right at the very moment (for Mynster had already nodded toward Goldschmidt but had not yet linked him with me) when I (out of love for my idea and the truth but also genuinely out of love for the old man) had once more lined up against the numerical and had broken sharply with Rudelbach and the Old Orthodox.

x⁴ A 552   n.d., 1852

To Declare Maieutically That One Himself Is Not a Christian

Take the Socratic position: error and evil are puffed-up knowledge—therefore Socrates is the ignorant one and remains that until the end. Likewise, to be a Christian has become an illusion, all these millions of Christians—therefore the situation must be reversed and Christianity must be introduced by a person who says that he himself is not a Christian.

This is the way I have understood it. But to what extent ought this tactic be maintained to the end, and to what extent should I stick to it?

For me the entire operation has been a matter of being honest with myself: whether and to what extent I wanted to become a Christian in the strictest sense. Devoutly (for I felt myself to be ordained to this task, my only one) I intellectually assumed the task of making clear what Christianity is, and the pseudonym[45] also declared himself not to be Christian.

But when the one who enters upon this operation is himself in the situation of having to determine whether he actually wants to become a Christian in the strictest sense, this tactic cannot and ought not to be maintained to the end. Otherwise the most appalling thing that could happen—that by screwing up the price of being a Christian he ultimately (let us take the extreme) would get everyone to give up Christianity and he himself would give it up. Furthermore, such a person, himself detached, could take a demonic delight in torturing those who call themselves Christians by attaching to them heavy burdens which he himself has not yet taken up.

So it is with me. But suppose that someone else had undertaken the enterprise of maieutically introducing Christianity, declaring himself not to be a Christian, someone else who from the outset had in deepest inwardness made up his mind about being and wanting to be a Christian in the strictest sense—ought this maieutic position then be maintained to the end or is there not a difficulty here which is not present in the Socratic position? To be specific, Christianity teaches that a danger is involved, persecution goes along with confessing that one is a true Christian—this is no doubt evaded by the person who in introducing Christianity declares himself not to be a Christian. True enough, the evil in "Christendom" is precisely that all are Christians and thus there is no danger connected with calling oneself Christian but rather an advantage, and here again, in reverse, the danger might come through not wanting to declare oneself to be a Christian. Yet to this Christianity might reply: "Because there is no danger connected with being a Christian in the sense that these millions are Christian, I do not for that reason take back my word that suffering, mockery, and persecution are still to be expected if one genuinely wants to be a Christian and confesses to being one—and this you evade by introducing Christianity in such a way that you declare yourself not to be a Christian." And so it is, too. The scruples about claiming to be a Christian which I have expressed in a little essay *Armed Neutrality*, (because I do not want the point of contention to be my claim that "I am a Christian" but that "I know what Christianity is"), because of the fear that on judgment day God might say to me: You have dared to call yourself a Christian—these scruples are removed by what I have pointed out here, that on judgment day God could very well say to such a person: By declaring yourself not to be a Christian, you have evaded suffering for confessing that you are a Christian (with respect to Socrates, there was no ignominy etc. connected with calling himself wise, something he evaded by calling himself ignorant).

But let us suppose that the person who introduced Christianity maieutically (in order to get rid of the illusion, the notion of being Christian because one is living in Christendom), declaring himself not to be a Christian, let us suppose that he not only from the beginning made up his mind about wanting to be a Christian in the strictest sense but that he completely ordered his life (although continually declaring himself not to be a Christian) according to the requirements of Christianity concerning renunciation, dying to the world,* and lived in voluntary poverty and thereby was definitely exposed to the suffering and persecution which are inseparable and are essential Christianity—can he continue to the end with this formula: I am not a Christian? The answer to this must be: Christianity nevertheless always requires the confession of Christ, and yet the suffering he suffers may not necessarily be for Christ's sake; perhaps he could also be secretly proud of having no fellowship with other Christians.

If the formula "I am not a Christian" is to be maintained to the end, then it must be done by an "apostle" but in an entirely new style. He must have an immediate relation to Christ and then only in death explain how it all hangs together. Whether or not this will ever happen, I cannot say.

  * *In margin*: and everything involved in "imitation," dying to the world, being born again, and so on, which I myself was not aware of in 1848.

x⁴ A 553   n.d., 1852

At the very time I hurled myself against Rudelbach, particularly at the very time when, presupposing that Mynster would at least remain quiet, I was even prepared to signalize Mynster once again in parting—the very person who made it impossible (by introducing Goldschmidt the way he did), even though I really wanted to do it ever so much—this person was Mynster himself.[46]

x⁴ A 606   n.d., 1852

> *Is it the law that I proclaim?*
> *Do I, myself in anxiety, perhaps want*
> *to bring anxiety upon others?*

In truth, no. See for yourself!

Imagine a government which from generation to generation cancelled a debt of 100,000 dollars which each inhabitant of the state owed—well, we can imagine it!

It went on like this from generation to generation—unchanged. But although this was unchanged, a change nevertheless took place. From generation to generation people grew more and more accustomed to this unchanged arrangement, so that finally—well, they did not deny that a debt had been cancelled—it made no greater impression upon them than if it had been four shillings which had been cancelled. If someone then said: No, it should not be like this. In fairness to our benefactor it ought to become clear how great the debt is—how great his benefaction. And it is to the recipient's interest to become properly aware of the greatness of the debt—and of the benefaction. It is in the recipient's interest that his gratitude might really be proportionate to the gift.

If someone did that, would this be an attempt to make himself and others anxious about how they could ever possibly repay this debt? No, this would not be what he is doing.

From a Christian point of view, it is the same with "grace." In fairness to God it ought to become clear how great the guilt is— but then it must first be made clear how great the requirement is. And it is to man's interest that this happen, so that his gratitude in no way has to be proportionate to the infinite greatness of merciful love [but to the greatness of the guilt forgiven by that infinite merciful love].

Tell me, is this severe, anxiety-creating? Would it not rather have been a sin against you not to make you aware, so that you seemed to be a much more ungrateful person than you are? In resentment you might sometime cry woe unto me and everyone who could have and should have made you aware but instead contributed to your remaining what in your innermost heart you are not—an ingrate—for this you are not.

XI² A 367   n.d., 1854-55

Gregor Malantschuk

COMMENTARY ON
ARMED NEUTRALITY
AND
AN OPEN LETTER

THE CONTENT OF
ARMED NEUTRALITY

Kierkegaard begins by pointing out why he uses the expression *armed neutrality*. We note that he simply states that he had already taken the position of armed neutrality and also that he "intend[s] to take" it in the future. In effect, Kierkegaard announces here a wait-and-see position toward his contemporaries until he has seen how his communication of "what Christianity is, or, more accurately, what is involved in being a Christian" has been received, and he prepares for two possibilities, either that of continuing to be neutral or that of making later use of his weapons. An obvious reference to "making admission and confession concerning himself" with regard to his distance from true Christianity was later made in *Training in Christianity*[1] in 1850, by which time Kierkegaard had decided not to publish *Armed Neutrality*, which lay finished in 1849.[2]

Kierkegaard clearly understood that his presentation of what it means to be a true Christian can be regarded only as an ideal, one by which his own life must also be judged. It was very important for Kierkegaard to emphasize this particular point in order to avoid running the risk of being regarded as one who is "a Christian to

an extraordinary degree, a remarkable kind of Christian." From
an entry in his journals it is clear that Kierkegaard thought he had
done everything needed to avert this misunderstanding. He says
that finally, in *Armed Neutrality*, "every misunderstanding" based
on the notion that he was an "apostle"[3] has been forestalled as decisively as possible." This kind of misunderstanding very likely
could be occasioned by the circumstance that Kierkegaard presented a new and more rigorous conception of Christianity which
could produce the impression that he not only thought he knew
Christianity better than his contemporaries but also considered
himself to be a better Christian. After having forestalled these mis-
understandings, he acknowledges the special qualifications he has
been given to enable him "to present a picture of a Christian in
all its ideality—that is, the true form and stature worked out to the
very last detail."

On the one hand, the position of "armed neutrality" required
him to communicate his insights to his contemporaries temper-
ately, but on the other hand it showed that, in case of attack, a
whole arsenal of weapons stood ready for the defense of this position. This conception of armed neutrality is expressed in a journal
entry of about the same time: "From my side let it be gentle—but
if they want a fight, I have good weapons in reserve."[4]

This temperateness is discernible in the beginning of the next
portion (p. 34 above), in which Kierkegaard admits that "it is an
overstatement to say that Christianity in our time has been completely abolished. No, Christianity is still present and in its truth,
but as a *teaching*, as *doctrine*." But even though Christianity is
present as objective truth, this is not the same as its actually being
present. Kierkegaard thereby distinguishes sharply between Christianity as an objective teaching and the subjective appropriation
of it. It is the latter he thinks his contemporaries lack. To need a
guide line for one's life and at the same time to be unwilling to
practice in existence the Christianity confessed as doctrine factually
places a person outside the sphere of Christianity.

˙ This flight from a personal appropriation of Christianity occurs, more particularly, in three ways (pp. 34-35).

(1) The polemical stance of Christianity toward the world is forgotten. In this way the tension between the single individual and the world vanishes. The result is the idolization of the *status quo*, leading to relaxation and excluding internal struggle within oneself and external struggle with the world; but only this struggle yields a true Christian outlook. "Relaxed piety," however, according to Kierkegaard, is "Jewish piety."

(2) In his discussion of the second form of the perversion of Christianity, Kierkegaard enters into the whole question of the contrast between knowledge and faith, something which occupied him especially because of Hegelian philosophy. First of all he gives his view of this large issue in the very abstractly formulated statement: "Every decisive qualification of being Christian is according to a dialectic or is on the other side of a dialectic." Since we find many analogous expressions in Kierkegaard, especially in his journals and papers, it is appropriate to explain here what Kierkegaard means by this statement. By the expression "dialectic" Kierkegaard means that a person cannot relate himself immediately or spontaneously or directly to Christianity. Reflection must always go before. Christ is called "the sign of contradiction."[5] This in itself sets reflection in motion, but the concepts "sin," "offense," etc., also presuppose reflection. Only after casting personal existence into reflection or, as Kierkegaard says, "on the other side of a dialectic" can a person achieve a new immediacy or spontaneity. Kierkegaard has formulated this relationship in the following way: ". . . faith . . . is spontaneity after reflection."[6] Reflection, therefore, is a condition for coming to Christianity, but it is not properly a point of arrival and rest; according to Kierkegaard one must risk the leap into the new spontaneity or immediacy, which is Christianity. The main error of Hegel and his followers was the belief that by knowledge (or as Kierkegaard would say, by reflection) it is possible to remove the opposition between the eternal and the temporal and

to regard this position as being higher than that of faith. This line of thought or, more particularly, Hegel's philosophy, can thus undermine the sphere of faith at certain points: first by obliterating the absolute distinction between faith and knowledge, and then by attempting to elevate knowledge above faith, and finally by placing emphasis upon the objective, the conceptual, without understanding the significance of the single individual, the existing subject. But all genuine reality is linked only to single, individual, existing persons. Kierkegaard expresses it by saying: "to exist (the single individual) consists of the dialectical element. . . ." This, again, means that the contradiction of existence which reflection discovers on the way to Christianity will create a tension in the individual's life which will continue throughout time.

(3) With regard to the appropriation of Christianity, since stress has been put upon the conceptual, the philosophical, the theoretical, "existence and the ethical" have been forgotten. In this way a perversion of Christianity takes place. By stressing the ethical as a condition for Christian existence, Kierkegaard is consistent with the substance of his published works, which can be characterized briefly by a quotation from the journals: "Ethics, or, better, the ethical, is the turning point, and from there the movement is into dogmatics."[7] Through the ethical, which teaches a person his own impotence, the way is prepared for the acceptance of Christ's gift of salvation.

Under these three points, then, Kierkegaard points to the relationships which were unfavorable to the process of appropriating Christianity. In the next portion he very concentratedly points out the nature of the positive counter needed against these negative tendencies.

It is clear from the following declaration (p. 35) that he considered his thoughts concerning this new and positive counter to be of essential importance: "From the very beginning my work has not been a labor of haste, has not been an impetuous amendment to the wholesale confusion or a new patch on an old garment."

In the next passage (pp. 35-36) Kierkegaard goes more deeply

into the substance of his effort. First he designates the various ap-
proaches used in his works in carrying out the task of presenting
"the ideal picture of being a Christian." Thereupon, as a parenthetical statement over a page long, Kierkegaard gives in very concen-
trated form important disclosures about his positive effort and an
explanation of the need for this effort. He organizes his communication in four clearly defined points.

From the beginning, in order to avert all misunderstanding of
what is developed later, the first point is established—namely, that
Christ is "much more than the prototype; he is the object of faith."
In other words, Kierkegaard stresses the work of salvation as the
most important goal of Christ's earthly life. We find this stress upon
Christ as the object of faith again at the end of the portion (p. 36).

After having made certain that his view of Christianity on this
most important point cannot be misunderstood, Kierkegaard turns
to the next point—specifically, that aspect of Christ's life which
Kierkegaard says engrosses him especially—Christ as the prototype.

Kierkegaard alleges that in Scripture Christ is "presented chiefly"
as "the object of faith." But this means that we actually know Christ
only in terms of his "being," that is, he meets us as master or as
one who without wavering goes his predetermined way; on the
other hand, we know less of Christ in terms of his "becoming," that
is, of his battle as that single individual with his earthly problems
in relation to the state, family life, etc.; and yet Kierkegaard thinks
that this could be of utmost importance to know for one who "has
earnestly sought to order his life according to his example." We
know that Kierkegaard had already been decisively occupied with
this and that he had called it one of "the most difficult of all problems."[8] In the journal entry about this Kierkegaard says that
"Christ's life has a negative-polemical relationship to Church and
state." And later in the same entry he says: "It would be the highest ethical paradox if God's Son entered into the whole of actuality,
became part of it, submitted to all of its triviality; for even if I have
the courage and trust and faith to die of starvation, this is worthy
of admiration, and in each generation there probably are not ten

who have it, but all the same we teach and proclaim that it would be even greater to submit to the actualities of life."

Kierkegaard had tried to solve these difficult questions regarding Christ as prototype, and his treatment of the issues appears in various places in his writings.

In the portion before us now, Kierkegaard sets forth the main point of what he had outlined as the solution of this question. He speaks specifically of "the middle terms" in relation to becoming a Christian. By "middle terms" (which according to Kierkegaard are lacking in the Biblical presentation of Christ) he understands a characterization of all the existential levels which a human being must go through if he wants Christ as the prototype of his life.

At the same time that Christ always remains "the object of faith" for a person, the middle terms will be able to assist him to clarity in his striving to use Christ's earthly existence as the model for his life. Kierkegaard calls the eliciting of these middle links, which describe the human pilgrimage which has Christ as the prototype, as "a kind of human interpreting of Christ as the prototype."

According to human interpreting of Christ's earthly life men are "derivatives," that is, as created beings and as links in the great coherence of the human race, they are placed face to face with an existential task. The task for every single individual thus becomes: from his given position and through definite existential levels to approach Christ as the prototype. In Kierkegaard's language the prompting to this spiritual process is called an attempt to cast "everything into becoming."

The phrase "casts everything into becoming" (p. 36) also shows that Kierkegaard does not want to give a new objective presentation of a decisive side of Christianity but wants to characterize the way of "inward deepening," in which the subjective element again comes to play an essential role. In *Armed Neutrality* Kierkegaard did not need to go into this more deeply, since he considered an extensive account to have been given in his works. It must be added here, however, that according to Kierkegaard's understanding, only by stressing Christ as the prototype will the most central truth of Christianity, Christ as the object of faith, come to have its full and proper place.

In the conclusion of this important portion (p. 36) Kierkegaard shows that the ideal picture he sketches will change, or as he puts it, will "modify," the conception of what it means to be a Christian. Kierkegaard considers that with his life and writings he had fashioned the needed "modification." In his attempt to change the common conception, Kierkegaard removed not only the errors of his age but of earlier periods. This he calls "modifications related to past confusions of a particular time."

By this brief parenthetical account Kierkegaard gives the main lines of the way he desired to serve Christianity.

In the pages following (pp. 36-39), Kierkegaard shows what qualifications are required in one who is to set forth the ideal picture of a Christian. Besides having dialectical and poetic powers, sober-mindedness and steadiness, he should not let himself be misled by enthusiastic followers into singling himself out as the prototype. Kierkegaard makes it perfectly clear that the presentation of a true Christian which he gives in his works must be regarded as an ideal, one by which a person must let himself first of all be judged and humbled. Only in this way, he is convinced, can the single individual be stimulated into striving toward the ideal.

Kierkegaard requires this attitude first and foremost of himself when he says: "The one who presents this ideal must be the very first one to humble himself under it, and even though he himself is striving within himself to approach this ideal, he must confess that he is very far from being it." Therefore Kierkegaard will not set himself up as the judge of others.[9] Every individual, "in quiet solitariness," ought to "compare his own life with the ideal." In this way the "inward deepening" which Kierkegaard regarded as the most important and stressed so strongly can begin for the individual.

Quite significantly, in his emphasis upon the importance of the single individual for the renewal of Christianity, Kierkegaard uses for the only time, as far as I know, the term "reformation" as descriptive of his activity (p. 38). That the stress in his "idea of a reformation" is placed upon the contribution of the individual is seen also in his drawing upon two ideas from *Works of Love*. The first is that the "whirling or the giddiness" which the modern man suffers because of the disintegration of values can be halted only by the single individual's decision to relate himself to the unconditional. The second is that the way to this absolute relationship involves the exclusion of all comparison with others. Such comparison would reduce the decision again to the level of finitude; the infinite quality of the resolution is lost when the quantitative "more or less" of comparison enters in.[10]

Kierkegaard's next observations (pp. 39-42) pertain again to his own position in regard to the ideal picture of a Christian. He has repudiated the notion of himself as being this outstanding Christian, but he now raises the question of how he dares associate himself with the idea of martyrdom. He speaks of this in the following way: "I would not dare, particularly not in Christendom, to expose myself to becoming a martyr, to being persecuted, to losing my life because I am a Christian." In developing this position Kierkegaard touches upon the whole complex of questions which he had treated, prior to writing *Armed Neutrality*, in the essay "Has a Man the Right to Let Himself Be Put to Death for the Truth?"[11]

In various journal entries[12] it is apparent that Kierkegaard had reflected upon the idea of martyrdom in relation to his own existence. As far as he himself was concerned, he had to answer this excruciating question, and he interweaves some traces of this answer in *Armed Neutrality*.

In his discussion of the idea of martyrdom (pp. 39-41) Kierkegaard emphasizes that on the part of the one involved it presupposes the free decision of willing to become a martyr; therefore it presupposes that the person himself exposes himself to the danger. To that extent the single individual himself decides and not "the others." Consequently the single individual himself in this way takes responsibility for the martyrdom. As long as one does not reflect upon this responsibility, the idea of martyrdom can appear to be only a question of the individual's courage and willingness to be sacrificed. But Kierkegaard shows that the whole problem is rendered difficult precisely by reflection upon the responsibility. By these reflections, Kierkegaard says, the idea of martyrdom is brought into relation with "inward deepening." Therefore martyrdom can be regarded from two points of view, which he characterizes in the following way (p. 41): "The more inwardness there is, the greater the fear and trembling before God. Externally oriented thinking is preoccupied with having the courage before men to become a martyr; inwardly oriented thinking is preoccupied with having the courage before God to be a martyr."

The outcome of Kierkegaard's reflections is that martyrdom, too, as the highest expression of Christian existence, must be conceived in a more rigorous and more inward way than generally had been done previously.

It is entirely in order, therefore, that right here (p. 41), where the idea of martyrdom is set in a qualitatively new definition, Kierkegaard introduces some observations which can properly be regarded as a proposal for Christendom's confession of its remoteness from the Christian ideal.

Kierkegaard elucidates this proposal for a confession by what he calls "a secular analogy" taken from philosophy, therefore from that knowledge and wisdom which seeks on a human basis to give an explanation of existence and its meaning. Kierkegaard points to the self-knowledge out of which some so-called wise men (σοφοι) in Greece decided to call themselves by the more modest name, friends or lovers of wisdom (φιλοσοφοι) and asks whether this change is to be regarded as "a step backward or a step forward." He himself thinks that it was a step forward when, perceiving the immensity of the task, they found a more modest expression.

We can see from Kierkegaard's journals that he had tried to apply this analogy to the current situation in Christendom. He wanted an admission to be made, in one way or another, of Christendom's distance from what he understood by true Christianity. It is interesting that Kierkegaard went so far as to transfer this analogy verbally to the Christian relationship; in a few entries he uses "lovers of Christ" as analogous to "lovers of wisdom." ". . . I believe that we are coming to characterize ourselves as Christ-lovers, because to be a Christian has become too great a task. Childlike simplicity did not observe what an infinite requirement is involved in being a Christian; therefore they could believe it was possible. Now it is apparent that the requirement for being a Christian is so enormous that humanness becomes satisfied with a relationship to it, a striving toward it."[13]

Obviously Kierkegaard does not mean that a new characterization would help make the achievement possible, but for him the point is to indicate an understanding of the greatness of the task and of the distance from the ideal.

In the last pages of *Armed Neutrality* (pp. 42ff.) Kierkegaard adds something of a more personal nature with reference to the portrayal of the "ideal picture of a Christian." He considers that he has "to an unusual degree . . . the qualifications" for portraying "with uncommon clarity and definiteness what Christianity is." We note that on this occasion, as on so many others, Kierkegaard says that credit for the way he had developed his capacities belonged to his father.[14]

He declares further that even though he dare not presume to expose himself to martyrdom as a Christian in an eminent sense, he is prepared, without avoiding "any danger," to uphold his portrayal of "what it means to be a Christian."

Thereafter (p. 43) Kierkegaard points out that his position would be a different one if he were in a pagan country. Then he would have to confess that he was a Christian. If he did this among men who already call themselves Christians, it would mean that he regarded himself as a special Christian in contrast to all the others, but this is precisely what he does not want to do. Therefore he takes a neutral stance, which he will maintain until the eventuality that his views are attacked.

Concerning his portrayal of the ideal Christian viewed in a larger perspective, Kierkegaard writes (p. 44), "This is my idea of the judgment which I believe is going to fall upon Christendom: Not that I or any single individual shall judge others, but the ideal picture of what it is to be a Christian will judge me and everyone who permits himself to be judged." Here it clearly appears that Kierkegaard expected an admission from individuals concerning their distance from the ideal.

Kierkegaard says further (p. 44) that it is accidental that he came to be the one to give the portrayal of the true Christian, but someone had to do it. Such a labor is rewarded with ingratitude in the degree to which it is done well. On the one hand, therefore, Kierkegaard maintains that a portrayal can be given of what the ideal Christian is—and this he himself had done; on the other hand he cautions the individual regarding his own ideas concerning himself as a Christian, since no man can know himself completely and decide with certainty to what extent he is rightly related to the truth. This is expressed in the last sentences of *Armed Neutrality*: "Nevertheless, it is still possible, perhaps, by continuous diligence over a number of years to pursue this to the point of *knowing* definitely what it means to be a Christian; whether one himself is that cannot be *known*, surely not *with definiteness*—it must be believed, and in faith there is always fear and trembling."

In the work *Armed Neutrality* Kierkegaard has consistently affirmed and carried through the position that for him the main thing has not been to determine *what* Christianity is, the objective aspect of Christianity, but to characterize *how* a person *becomes a Christian*. This concern for the way objective truth becomes an actuality in a subject is the main motivation for all the rest of Kierkegaard's writings.

THE SIGNIFICANCE OF
AN OPEN LETTER

Søren Kierkegaard did not want to use the word "reformation" for his efforts as a religious philosopher in the service of Christianity. The word "reformation"[15] is usually associated either with a change in external ecclesiastical relations or with a rectification of certain tenets of Christian doctrine. This change is therefore primarily objective in character and based on the conviction that it is accomplished essentially merely by renovating the structure of the Church or by putting a more Bible-centered emphasis on particular tenets. Kierkegaard takes a path opposite to that of the reformers. The essential thing for him is not the objective organization of the Church or the *what* of Christian doctrine, but the subjective, that is, the *how*. This means that Kierkegaard concentrates wholly upon the inner reality of the single individual and regards change within him as the most important factor for Christian existence.

In order to avoid misunderstanding, therefore, Kierkegaard, from the very beginning of his authorship, maintained the tactic of avoiding all expressions which could be interpreted as a proposal for external change. Thus, when the learned theologian A. G. Rudelbach, in his book *On Civil Marriage* (1851) cited Kierkegaard's name in support of his efforts for the emancipation of the Church from the state and for the "introduction of the institution of civil marriage,"[16] since according to Rudelbach's understanding Kierkegaard, too, was opposed to "*habitual* and *legally-established Christianity*,"[17] Kierkegaard felt prompted to protest. To Kierkegaard it was clear that if he remained silent he would be in danger of being exploited in the interest of a certain trend in the ecclesiastical controversy involving Rudelbach and many others at the time.

Under the circumstances, Kierkegaard wanted to continue to preserve his independent position and did not wish to enter into controversy over externals, particularly since for him the main issue now and always was to show that "ideality with respect to being Christian means a continual inward deepening."[18]

It is of interest to note that in his letter of protest against Rudelbach in *The Fatherland*, Kierkegaard first of all (p. 47, above) reproaches Rudelbach for lumping all of his writings, including the "numerous, qualitatively different pseudonymous works" as well as the "variegated edifying or upbuilding works," under the name Søren Kierkegaard. Kierkegaard wants a distinction to be made between the positions in his individual works. Yet, however different these works might be, he nevertheless insists that none of them contains a proposal for external changes in the sphere of the Church (p. 49).

Kierkegaard then goes on (pp. 49-51) to emphasize forcefully how he had worked toward establishing the inward deepening of Christianity in the individual as the main task for himself and others. Since "Christianity is inwardness, inward deepening," a Christian is free to live under various external situations and Christianity must in no way be mixed up with politics as Rudelbach attempted to do. The "free institutions" which Rudelbach battled for may have their significance for the state but not for Christianity, which is "infinitely higher and infinitely freer than all institutions, constitutions, etc." Kierkegaard then names martyrdom as the way Christianity, if the need arises, takes its proper stance in this world (p. 51).[19]

Kierkegaard is, as he ironically says of himself (p. 50), a Christian simpleton or Christian-dumb (*christendum*),[20] and he must leave it to others to occupy themselves with the relation between Church and state. There is also a certain irony in the fact that Kierkegaard, who insists that he himself is concerned for the essential aspect of Christianity and thereby indirectly declares that Rudelbach is occupied with the unessential, speaks so approvingly of Rudelbach at the same time he minimizes himself (p. 51): "Dr. R. possesses amazing learning; as far as I know he is probably the most learned man in Denmark, and in my opinion we all ought to be happy to have such a learned man among us. On the other hand, in learning and scholarship, I am, especially by comparison, a poor bungler who knows enough arithmetic for household use."

Finally, Kierkegaard gives two examples of how a Christian may be constrained to stand up in opposition to external situations and thereby actually influence their change without having aimed at this primarily. The first example (pp. 52-53) is taken from Acts 5:29, concerning the apostle Peter's consulting with God and disobeying the official order not to proclaim the gospel.

The second example (p. 54) is taken from the life of Luther, his entering into marriage with Katharina von Bora despite his monastic vow, after having consulted "God and his conscience."

It must be added that even before the publication of his rebuke of Rudelbach Kierkegaard was entirely clear as to how different their respective views of Christianity were. Contributing especially to this clarity was Rudelbach's book on the origin and principle of the constitution of the Protestant Church.[21] With particular reference to this book Kierkegaard wrote the following:

"Dr. Rudelbach and I

"We shall never understand one another.

"For him it has long since been definitely settled that he is a Christian. And now he busies himself with history and the external forms of the Church. He has never felt the disquietude of the idea, wondering every single day whether he is now a Christian or not. 'Never'—no, because one who has felt this once, one day, one hour, does not let go of it during his entire life, or it never lets go of him.

"The idea has involved me in personal self-concern, and therefore I can never find time for projects, for I must begin every day with this concern: Are you a Christian now? Indeed, perhaps this very day there will be an existential collision which will make it clear that you are not a Christian at all."[22]

Thus Rudelbach's books became an external provocation for Kierkegaard to become quite concerned in his journals with what he considered a harmful interest in a new reformation or zeal to play the role of reformer. He knew that his writings had dampened this zeal for reforming. Among other things he wrote: "Nevertheless, I hope that there will be no reformation. Just as Napoleon cleared the hall with his grenadiers, so a poet will come who will clear it with the aid of ideals."[23] This poet was Kierkegaard himself.

Rudelbach, of course, could not let Kierkegaard's rebuke go

unanswered. In two issues of *The Fatherland* (Nos. 37 and 38, 1851) he replied to Kierkegaard's objections. In the first article he shows at how many points he agrees with "his honored friend," Søren Kierkegaard. But in the second article he tries to show that Christians had always formed congregations and were not merely single individuals. "*The single individual* never wants to be *alone* when he witnesses, acts, or suffers for God's cause but wants continually to be surrounded by a *cloud of witnesses* (Hebrews 12:1), even when outwardly he seems to be most forsaken; he never wants to go forth in the service of the spirit and of the word without having the net which the Lord first consecrated for Peter for the catching of men."[24]

Relevant to this, Kierkegaard comments as follows: "Very true, many joined the apostle. But it was not a case of the apostle consulting with them *first*, counting how many there were, and agreeing on some plan of action with them. No, he initiated his action—period; and it was then that many joined up, profiting from the fact that the apostle had acted. When Rudelbach (in the article in *The Fatherland*) talks about the apostle being surrounded by a cloud of witnesses, he surely is mistaken, for he sees the cloud—and not the apostle."[25]

In Kierkegaard's subsequent writings as well, inward deepening was emphasized as the most important and most essential aspect of Christianity, but in the end he apparently approached Rudelbach's position, for during the Church controversy he directed his charges not only against the Church but also against the state. But for Kierkegaard the critique of the state proceeded from different motives and rested upon a completely different basis than was the case with Rudelbach, who, like Grundtvig, accepted a position as a state official at the same time that he fought for greater freedom of the Church in relation to the state. In one of his journal entries from the time just before the Church controversy, Kierkegaard declares: "Rudelbach (and also Grundtvig) cry out that it is the state-Church which ruins Christianity—and both of them remain in their positions in the state-Church. Grundtvig takes the most desirable position in the whole country, and R. gets a huge salary."[26]

In relation to the state, Kierkegaard never wanted to assert the right to form free ecclesiastical institutions. The basis of his indictment of the state was that by its general encompassing of the lives of Christians in organized forms and by its support of these forms it contributed to making Christianity entirely external and superficial. Thus the individual is more easily enabled to slip out of the inner decisions and battles which characterize Christianity. Kierkegaard did, in fact, remain true to the end to his conviction that "Christianity is inwardness, inward deepening."

FOR REFERENCE

CHRONOLOGICAL TABLE
BIBLIOGRAPHY
ABBREVIATIONS AND NOTES
GUIDE TO "SELECTED ENTRIES"
INDEX

CHRONOLOGICAL TABLE*

1848-1851

Pertaining

to Armed Neutrality *and*

An Open Letter

1848

January

"Concerning Joyful Notes in the Strife of Suffering,"
Part II of *Christian Discourses* (VIII¹ A 500, 504).

January 25

Nord og Syd, Vol. I, No. 2, ed. M. Goldschmidt.

February 11

Plans for *Thoughts Which Cure Radically*, to include *The Sickness unto Death* (VIII¹ A 558).

April 19

"My whole nature is changed . . . I am free to speak"
(VIII¹ A 640).

April 24

"No, no, my reserve still cannot be broken, at least
not now" (VIII¹ A 645).

---

* See page 159, Abbreviations and Notes, for an explanation of references to
Kierkegaard's *Papirer (Journals and Papers)*.

April 26

Christian Discourses, by S. Kierkegaard, published.

May

Journal entries on forgiveness and faith
(VIII[1] A 646-50, 665, 673).

May 15

Journal NB[5] [IX A 1] begun.

Entry on imitation, prompted by reading in A. G. Rudelbach, *Christelig Biographie* (IX A 7, 49).

Idea of a new pseudonym: Anticlimacus (IX A 9).

July 16

Journal NB[6] [IX A 152] begun.
Entry on indirect method (IX A 171).
A penitent (IX A 172).

July 26-27

The Crisis and a Crisis in the Life of an Actress, by Inter et Inter, in four parts in *Fædrelandet (The Fatherland)*, Nos. 188-91.

August

Plan for a periodical *Armed Neutrality* to present a "definite and non-reduplicated idea of what I myself mean, what I am aiming at," and consideration of second edition of *Either/Or* (IX A 212).

Reflections on indirect and direct communication (IX A 218, 221-24, 233-35, 260, 392; see also IX B 57, X[3] A 413).

Thought of death, but "Rasmus Nielsen . . . can provide explanation [of the works]" (IX A 219, 220).

Relations with Professor Rasmus Nielsen (IX A 228-31).

August 21

Journal NB⁷ [IX A 252] begun.

November

"The Point of View for My Work as an Author . . . as good as finished" (IX A 293).

Consideration of publishing *Armed Neutrality* together with *The Sickness unto Death,* "Come Hither All Ye," and "Blessed Is He Who Is Not Offended" in a single volume under the title, *The Collected Works of Completion* or perhaps . . . *of Consummation* (IX A 390).

November 26

Journal NB⁸ [IX A 376] begun.

Entries on "upbringing," the martyr as teacher, the single individual, and an age of disintegration (IX B 63: 11-13, B 64, B 66).

Armed Neutrality possibly together with *Training in Christianity* (X⁵ B 105).

Armed Neutrality possibly an appendix to *The Point of View* (X⁵ B 106, 108-10).

1849

January 2

Journal NB⁹ [X¹ A 1] begun.

Entry on the publishing of *Armed Neutrality* and other works (X¹ A 74).

Misgivings about publishing *The Point of View for My Work as an Author* (X¹ A 78, 79).

February 9

Journal NB¹⁰ [X¹ A 81] begun.

Armed Neutrality characterizes as accurately as possible the "poetic attempt—without authority" (X[1] A 97).

Entry on preaching in a situation of actuality (X[1] A 136).

Entry on imitation and prototype (X[1] A 132-35).

March

Entry on "stepping forth in character" (X[1] A 138, etc.).

Reference to seminary appointment in conversation with Mynster (X[1] A 167).

Renewed reflections on indirect communication (X[1] A 235)

"Dialectical as my nature is" (X[1] A 246).

April

"The Accounting," a concentration from *The Point of View*, written but not to be published (X[1] A 266).

Only a poet, but considering "stepping forth in character"; economic concerns (X[1] A 273).

April 25

Entry on the poet and the religious life (X[1] A 281).

May 2

Journal NB[11] [X[1] A 295] begun.

May 4

Decision to publish "Has a Man the Right to Let Himself Be Put to Death for the Truth?" and "Of the Difference Between a Genius and an Apostle" by H. H. (X[1] A 302).

May 14

Second edition of *Either/Or* published; *The Lilies of the Field and the Birds of the Air*, by S. Kierkegaard, published.

May 19

Two Minor Ethical-Religious Treatises, by H. H., published (see May 4, 1849 above).

June 4

Reflections concerning pseudonymity and the publishing of *Armed Neutrality*, *The Point of View*, *The Sickness unto Death*, *A Cycle of Ethical-Religious Essays*, and the three works "Come Hither All Ye," "Blessed Is He Who Is Not Offended," "From on High He Will Draw," possibly under title *Training in Christianity* (X^1 A 422).

Change of plans; on impatience and financial concern (X^1 A 424).

Possibility of publishing *Armed Neutrality* together with *Training in Christianity* (X^1 A 450).

June 24, 25

Entry on "stepping forth in character" (X^1 A 494, 499).

On being a poet and the question of "going out beyond my limits." "But nothing about my personality as a writer; it is false to want to anticipate during one's lifetime—this merely converts a person into the interesting" (X^1 A 510).

June 26

Death of Regine Olsen's father.

July 19

Journal NB[12] [X^1 A 542] begun.

July 30

> *The Sickness unto Death*, by Anti-Climacus, edited
> by S. Kierkegaard, published.

August 31

> *Den evangeliske Kirkeforfatnings Oprindelse og
> Princip*, by Dr. A. G. Rudelbach (a work on the con-
> stitution of the Church), published (X^1 A 660, 669).

September 28

> Journal NB^{13} [X^2 A 69] begun.

October

> "For the postscript to The Accounting" (X^5 B 205).
>
> Characterization of the new pseudonym Anti-Clima-
> cus (X^2 A 147, 177, X^5 B 206).
>
> Return by Fritz Schlegel of Kierkegaard's letter to
> Regine Olsen Schlegel (X^2 A 210).

November 9

> Journal NB^{14} [X^2 A 164] begun.

November 13

> *Three Discourses at the Communion on Fridays*, by
> S. Kierkegaard, published.

December 28

> *Aanden i Naturen (The Spirit in Nature)*, by Hans
> Christian Ørsted, published.
>
> Entry on imitation and collision (X^2 A 317).
>
> "A word concerning myself" (X^5 B 153).

1849-50

> "The interesting," idol or martyr of the moment,
> thorn in the flesh (X^5 B 249).

"Addition to 'The Accounting' " (X^5 B 255).

1850

January 6

Journal NB^{15} [X^2 A 329] begun.

February 14

Journal NB^{16} [X^2 A 468] begun.

Writings about himself and authorship cannot be published now; financial concerns (X^2 A 511).

March

Portion of draft of *For Self-Examination* (X^2 A 555-56).

March 6

Journal NB^{17} [X^2 A 574] begun.

April

"I would gladly accept an appointment—but my melancholy enters in and makes difficulties. . . ." (X^2 A 619).

Entry on reflection and decision (X^2 A 636).

"Freer relation desired" to Rasmus Nielsen (X^3 A 2).

May 5

Portion of draft of *For Self-Examination* (X^3 A 34).

May 15

Journal NB^{18} [X^3 A 44] begun.

On requirement and indulgence (X^3 A 72).

June 9

Journal NB^{19} [X^3 A 158] begun.

Reference to *Armed Neutrality* (X^3 A 204).

July 11

Journal NB[20] [X[3] A 254] begun.

On imitation and collision (X[3] A 283).

Concerning the unpublished writings (X[3] A 289).

On indirect and direct communication (X[3] A 413).

September

"*On My Work as an Author* must be held back yet" (X[3] A 423).

September 11

Journal NB[21] [X[3] A 438] begun.

September 27

Training in Christianity, by Anti-Climacus, published.

October 22

Conversation with Bishop Mynster after he had read *Training in Christianity* (X[3] A 563-64).

November 13

Journal NB[22] [X[3] A 611] begun.

December 20

An Edifying Discourse ("The Woman Who Was a Sinner"), by S. Kierkegaard, published.

1851

January

Om det borgerlige Ægteskab (On Civil Marriage), by A. G. Rudelbach, published.

January 19

"Mynster preached today on the beauty of the Christian life—and very beautifully" (X[3] A 782).

January 22

Journal NB[23] [X[4] A 1] begun.

"Dr. Rudelbach and I. We shall never understand one another" (X[4] A 20).

January 31

An Open Letter Prompted by a Reference to Me by Dr. Rudelbach, by S. Kierkegaard, *Fædrelandet (The Fatherland)*, No. 26.

Unpublished additions to *An Open Letter* (X[5] B 120-26).

February

On Rudelbach, political methods, and the Church (X[4] A 36, 37, 46).

"The present step against Rudelbach involves a double danger . . ." (X[4] A 79).

February 13, 14

A. G. Rudelbach's reply to *An Open Letter, Fædrelandet (The Fatherland)*, Nos. 37-38.

"The End of the Affair" (Rudelbach) (X[5] B 128).

On Rudelbach, Mynster, and official-culture-Christianity (X[4] A 126).

April 20

Journal NB[24] [X[4] A 240] begun.

May 2

Conversation with Bishop Mynster touching upon Rudelbach and Goldschmidt in relation to Bishop Mynster and the Church (X[4] A 270-72; see also X[4] A 552, 606).

Concerning the indirect method and *Armed Neutrality* (X⁴ A 553).

August 7

On My Work as an Author (including parts of *Armed Neutrality*), by S. Kierkegaard, published.

Two Discourses at the Communion on Fridays, by S. Kierkegaard, published.

August 9

Conversation with Bishop Mynster (X⁴ A 373).

Entry concerning Mynster, *Training in Christianity*, and Goldschmidt (X⁴ A 377).

September 10

For Self-Examination, Recommended for the Times, by S. Kierkegaard, published.

BIBLIOGRAPHY

Kierkegaard's Works in English
Translation

Editions referred to in the Notes.
Listed in order of first publication or time of writing.

The Concept of Irony, tr. Lee Capel. New York: Harper and Row, 1966; Bloomington: Indiana University Press, 1968. (*Om Begrebet Ironi*, by S. A. Kierkegaard, 1841.)

Either/Or, I, tr. David F. Swenson and Lillian Marvin Swenson; II, tr. Walter Lowrie; 2 ed. rev. Howard A. Johnson. Garden City: Doubleday, 1959. (*Enten-Eller*, I-II, ed. Victor Eremita, 1843.)

Johannes Climacus, or De omnibus dubitandum est, and *A Sermon*, tr. T. H. Croxall. London: Adam and Charles Black, 1958. ("Johannes Climacus eller De omnibus dubitandum est," written 1842-43, unpubl., *Papirer* IV B 1.)

Edifying Discourses, I-IV, tr. David F. Swenson and Lillian Marvin Swenson. Minneapolis: Augsburg Publishing House, 1943-46. (*Opbyggelige Taler*, by S. Kierkegaard, 1843, 1844.)

Fear and Trembling (with *The Sickness unto Death*), tr. Walter Lowrie. Garden City: Doubleday, 1954. (*Frygt og Bæven*, by Johannes de Silentio, 1843.)

Repetition, tr. Walter Lowrie. Princeton: Princeton University Press, 1941. (*Gjentagelsen*, by Constantine Constantius, 1843.)

Philosophical Fragments, tr. David Swenson, 2 ed. rev. Howard Hong. Princeton: Princeton University Press, 1962. (*Philoso-*

phiske Smuler, by Johannes Climacus, ed. S. Kierkegaard, 1844.)

Kierkegaard's The Concept of Dread [Anxiety], tr. Walter Lowrie. 2 ed., Princeton: Princeton University Press, 1944. (*Begrebet Angest*, by Vigilius Haufniensis, ed. S. Kierkegaard, 1844.)

Thoughts on Crucial Situations in Human Life, tr. David F. Swenson, ed. Lillian Marvin Swenson. Minneapolis: Augsburg Publishing House, 1941. (*Tre Taler ved tænkte Leiligheder*, by S. Kierkegaard, 1845.)

Stages on Life's Way, tr. Walter Lowrie. Princeton: Princeton University Press, 1940. (*Stadier paa Livets Vej*, ed. Hilarius Bogbinder, 1845.)

Kierkegaard's Concluding Unscientific Postscript, tr. David F. Swenson and Walter Lowrie. Princeton: Princeton University Press for American-Scandinavian Foundation, 1941. (*Afsluttende uvidenskabelig Efterskrift*, by Johannes Climacus, ed. S. Kierkegaard, 1846.)

The Present Age and *Two Minor Ethico-Religious Treatises*, tr. Alexander Dru and Walter Lowrie. London and New York: Oxford University Press, 1940. (*En literair Anmeldelse, To Tidsaldre*, by S. Kierkegaard, 1846; *Tvende ethisk-religieuse Smaa-Afhandlinger*, by H. H., 1849.)

On Authority and Revelation, The Book on Adler, tr. Walter Lowrie. Princeton: Princeton University Press, 1955. ("Bogen om Adler," written 1846-47, unpubl., *Papirer* VII² B 235.)

Purity of Heart, tr. Douglas Steere, 2 ed. New York: Harper, 1948. (*Opbyggelige Taler i forskjellig Aand*, by S. Kierkegaard, pt. 1, "En Leiligheds-Tale," 1847.)

The Gospel of Suffering and *The Lilies of the Field*, tr. David F. Swenson and Lillian Marvin Swenson. Minneapolis: Augsburg Publishing House, 1948. (*Opbyggelige Taler i forskjellig Aand*, by S. Kierkegaard, pt. 3, "Lidelsernes Evangelium"; pt. 2, "Hvad man lærer af Lilierne paa Marken og af Himmelens Fugle," 1847.)

Works of Love, tr. Howard and Edna Hong. New York: Harper and Row, 1962. (*Kjerlighedens Gjerninger*, by S. Kierkegaard, 1847.)

Crisis in the Life of an Actress, tr. Stephen Crites. New York: Harper and Row, 1967. ("Krisen og en Krise i en Skuespillerindes Liv," by Inter et Inter, *Fædrelandet,* Nos. 188-91, July 24-27, 1848.)

Christian Discourses, including also *The Lilies of the Field and the Birds of the Air* and *Three Discourses at the Communion on Fridays,* tr. Walter Lowrie. London and New York: Oxford University Press, 1939. (*Christelige Taler,* by S. Kierkegaard, 1848; *Lilien paa Marken og Fuglen under Himlen,* by S. Kierkegaard, 1849; *Tre Taler ved Altergangen om Fredagen,* by S. Kierkegaard, 1849.)

The Sickness unto Death (with *Fear and Trembling*), tr. Walter Lowrie. New York: Doubleday, 1954. (*Sygdommen til Døden,* by Anti-Climacus, ed. S. Kierkegaard, 1849.)

Training in Christianity, including also "The Woman Who Was a Sinner," tr. Walter Lowrie. London and New York: Oxford University Press, 1941; repr. Princeton: Princeton University Press, 1944. (*Indøvelsen i Christendom,* by Anti-Climacus, ed. S. Kierkegaard, 1850; *En opbyggelig Tale,* by S. Kierkegaard, 1850.)

Armed Neutrality and *An Open Letter,* tr. Howard V. Hong and Edna H. Hong. Bloomington and London: Indiana University Press, 1968 (the present volume). (*Den bevæbnede Neutralitet,* written 1848-49, publ. 1965; "Foranlediget ved en Yttring af Dr. Rudelbach mig betræffende," *Fædrelandet,* No. 26, January 31, 1851.)

The Point of View . . . , including "Two Notes about 'the Individual' " and *On My Work as an Author,* tr. Walter Lowrie. London and New York: Oxford University Press, 1939. (*Synspunktet for min Forfatter-Virksomhed,* by S. Kierkegaard, written 1848, publ. 1859; *Om min Forfatter-Virksomhed,* by S. Kierkegaard, 1851.)

For Self-Examination, tr. Edna and Howard Hong. Minneapolis: Augsburg Publishing House, 1940. (*Til Selvprøvelse,* by S. Kierkegaard, 1851.)

Judge for Yourselves! in *For Self-Examination* and *Judge for Your-*

selves! . . . , including also *Two Discourses at the Communion on Fridays* and *The Unchangeableness of God* (tr. David Swenson), tr. Walter Lowrie. Princeton: Princeton University Press, 1944. (*Dommer Selv!* by S. Kierkegaard, 1852; *To Taler ved Altergangen om Fredagen*, by S. Kierkegaard, 1851; *Guds Uforanderlighed*, by S. Kierkegaard, 1855.)

Kierkegaard's Attack upon "Christendom" 1854-1855, tr. Walter Lowrie. Princeton: Princeton University Press, 1944. (Bladartikler I-XXI, by S. Kierkegaard, *Fædrelandet*, 1854-55; *Dette skal siges, saa være det da sagt*, by S. Kierkegaard, 1855; *Øieblikket*, by S. Kierkegaard, 1-9, 1855; 10, 1905; *Hvad Christus dømmer om officiel Christendom*, by S. Kierkegaard, 1855.)

The Journals of Søren Kierkegaard . . . a Selection . . . , tr. Alexander Dru. London and New York: Oxford University Press, 1938. (From *Søren Kierkegaards Papirer*, I-XI¹ in 18 volumes, 1909-36.)

The Last Years, tr. Ronald C. Smith. New York: Harper and Row, 1965. (From *Papirer* XI¹-XI³, 1936-48.)

Søren Kierkegaard's Journals and Papers, tr. Howard V. Hong and Edna H. Hong. Bloomington and London: Indiana University Press, I, 1967; II-V in preparation. (From *Papirer* I-XI³, additional unpublished papers, and *Breve og Aktstykker vedrørende Søren Kierkegaard*, ed. Niels Thulstrup, I-II, 1953-54.)

At various times in recent years over twenty-five paperback editions of twenty Kierkegaard titles in English translation have appeared. For paperback editions currently available, see the latest issue of *Paperback Books in Print*, published by R. R. Bowker Co., 1180 Avenue of the Americas, New York, N. Y.

General works on Kierkegaard are listed in the Bibliography of *Søren Kierkegaard's Journals and Papers*, I, pp. 482-88. Studies of a more limited and specific nature are listed in the appropriate section of topical notes in each volume of *Søren Kierkegaard's Journals and Papers*.

ABBREVIATIONS
AND NOTES

S.V. refers to Kierkegaard's collected works (*Søren Kierkegaards Samlede Værker*, first edition, Copenhagen: 1901-6).

Page numbers following English titles of Kierkegaard's works refer to the translated editions listed in the Bibliography, page 155-58 above.

References with a Roman numeral, a capital A, B, or C, and an Arabic numeral (I A 31) refer to Kierkegaard's journals and papers (*Søren Kierkegaards Papirer*, I-XI³, Copenhagen: 1909-48). These papers (twenty volumes published in Danish, three more to come) consist of: journals (designated by A) which Kierkegaard kept for the latter half of his life; various other papers containing drafts, observations, and notations concerning his own works (designated by B); and notes on lectures and reading (designated by C). The references are given in the form used internationally (II A 770, VIII¹ A 558, X⁵ B 105, etc.). An extensive edition of selections in English translation is now in preparation for publication by the Indiana University Press; Volume I appeared in 1967.

Five periods denote an omission in the Danish text as it stands. Three periods denote an omission by the present editors. Brackets are used for material inserted in the text by the editors, or to enclose certain crucial Danish terms immediately following their English translation.

Footnote numbers in the text refer to the editors' notes, which appear at the end of the volume. Kierkegaard's notes and marginal comments appear at the bottom of the particular page, at the end of the entry, or in a few cases as an insertion within an entry.

SØREN KIERKEGAARD—POET OR PASTOR?

1. Without going into the collision between poet and pastor, Pastor Villads Christensen in his important book, *Søren Kierkegaard: Det cen-*

trale i hans Livssyn (The Crux of His View of Life), Copenhagen: 1964, in the section "A Ministry in the Spotlight," treats Kierkegaard's reflections on seeking a pastoral appointment.

2. VIII¹ A 42.

3. Poul M. Møller, *Efterladte Skrifter* (Copenhagen: 1843), III, p. 171.

4. X² A 277.

5. VIII¹ A 100.

6. I A 72.

7. T. F. Troels-Lund, *Bakkehus og Solbjerg* (Copenhagen: 1920-22), III, p. 135.

8. Hans Brøchner, *Erindringer om Søren Kierkegaard*, ed. Steen Johansen (Copenhagen: 1953), pp. 21 ff.

9. VII¹ A 221, *Papirer* VII¹, p. 145.

10. VIII¹ A 419.

11. VIII¹ A 422.

12. VI A 55.

13. VI A 59.

14. VI A 43.

15. See note 1 and also *Breve og Aktstykker vedrørende Søren Kierkegaard*, ed. Niels Thulstrup (Copenhagen: 1953), pp. 19 ff., and IV C 1 (terminal sermon).

16. IX A 213.

17. X⁵ A 146.

18. X⁵ B 217.

19. *Either/Or*, II, p. 281.

20. X⁵ A 146. See p. 31 above.

21. VII¹ A 4. See Bibliography, *The Present Age*.

22. VII¹ A 98, *Papirer* VII¹, p. 46.

23. VII¹ A 98.

24. X¹ A 558; also see X¹ A 316 and X⁴ A 673 (conclusion).

25. X¹ A 309.

26. Printed in English translation together with *The Present Age*, pp. 71-119.

27. VII¹ A 229.

28. See *Fear and Trembling*, pp. 38 ff.; *Works of Love*, pp. 59 ff.

29. X¹ A 11. For Kierkegaard's juxtaposing of thinkers and poets see VII¹ A 82.

30. VII¹ A 169.

31. X¹ A 476.

32. IV A 107, *Papirer* IV, p. 43.

33. VI A 43.

34. *The Sickness unto Death*, pp. 208-9.

35. VII¹ A 152.

36. X² A 98.

37. X¹ A 497.

38. X¹ A 498.

39. X¹ A 499.

40. X² A 177.

41. VIII² B 79-89. Under COMMUNICATION in *Søren Kierkegaard's Journals and Papers*, I.

42. X¹ A 167.

43. X⁴ A 218.

44. X⁴ A 373.

45. X⁴ A 604.

46. X⁴ A 673.

47. XI² A 12.

48. This is pointed out in *Two Discourses at the Communion on Fridays*, August, 1851, even though Kierkegaard published *For Self-Examination* a month later.

49. X⁵ A 105.

50. X⁵ A 89, *Papirer* X⁵, pp. 106 ff.

51. X² A 664.

52. X⁶ B 232, *Papirer* X⁶, p. 371.

53. VIII² B 85:18.

54. IX A 39.

55. X⁴ A 287.

56. XI³ B 120.

57. See Jørgen Bukdahl, *Søren Kierkegaard og den menige Mand* (Copenhagen: 1961).

58. XI² A 265.

INTRODUCTION TO
ARMED NEUTRALITY AND *AN OPEN LETTER*

1. *Den bevæbnede Neutralitet*, X⁵ B 107.

2. "Foranledigt ved en Yttring af Dr. Rudelbach mig betræffende," *Fædrelandet*, No. 26, January 31, 1851, *S.V.* XIII, pp. 436-44.

3. *Søren Kierkegaards Papirer*, ed. P. A. Heiberg, V. Kuhr, and E. Torsting, 20 vols., I-XI³ (Copenhagen: 1909-48).

4. *The Point of View*, p. 27.

5. Published in English with *The Present Age*. See Bibliography.

6. S. Kierkegaard, *Den bevæbnede Neutralitet*, ed. Gregor Malant-schuk (Copenhagen: 1965), pp. 9-10.

7. H. Martensen, *Af mit Levnet* (Copenhagen: 1883), I, pp. 23-24.

8. H. Martensen, *Leiligheds Taler* (Copenhagen: 1844), p. 20.

ARMED NEUTRALITY

1. The expression was used initially in international political life in 1780, when Denmark, Norway, and Russia, and subsequently Sweden, entered into an agreement in Copenhagen for the defense of their rights against the great powers, England in particular.

2. The qualifications according to psychical capacities, which vary from person to person, such as poetic or philosophical capacities. See IV C 96.

3. See I A 328. This theme is treated extensively in *The Present Age*.

4. In his later journal entries Kierkegaard compares Judaism and Christianity, particularly the Judaism and Christianity of his time. A note illustrating the latter is the following: "I continue to maintain that the little bit of piety which is in Christianity is Jewish piety (a tenacity for this life, a hope and a belief that God will bless them in this life, etc.; sure proof that God is one's friend is the fact that everything goes well in this world)—and they persist in appending Christ's name to this" (X² A 80).

5. Kierkegaard wrote three additional versions of this passage in his final draft for *Armed Neutrality*: (1) "For example, they say that to remain in the world is a higher form of life than the movement to the monastery, but does it follow from this that everyone who remains in the world has gone through the movement to the monastery?" (2) "But if this dialectic is not true, the outcome is not a return to the world but is pure and simple secularism; far from being abrogated, the dialectic has not been reached." (3) "But the entire dialectic in relation to being a Christian has been abrogated, through the influence of science, to the confusion of life, and thus being a Christian has been abrogated. The

monastic movement, for example (actual renunciation of the earthly), has thus been made into a purely abrogated movement. They falsely claim that everyone has quietly made this movement in his innermost being—and then they return to secularism" (X⁵ B 109).

6. The observation is directed against Hegel and all those who place knowledge above faith.

7. Proposal of change.

8. See Matthew 9:16 and Mark 2:21.

9. *various forms of pathos. Pathos* means passion or active concern. Here it means passionate interest in something, a passionate appropriation. Concerning the various forms of pathos see, for example, *Concluding Unscientific Postscript*, pp. 347 ff.

10. The existential stages, each with its own center. Thus God is the center in the "You shall" of the law's command and in that way is the fundamental middle term for man. See, for example, *Works of Love*, pp. 112-13: "Christianity teaches that love is a relationship between: man—God—man; that is, God is the middle term."

11. On comparison and ideality see *Works of Love*, pp. 121 ff. and 174 ff.

12. An incontrovertible, clear, convincing judgment or assertion.

13. Kierkegaard's definition is: "To reduplicate is to exist in what one understands." See *Training in Christianity*, p. 133. See also ibid., p. 123, and VIII A 91.

14. Kierkegaard names Pythagoras as the first to use the name "philosopher." He got his information from Diogenes Laertius, *Lives and Opinions of the Ancient Philosophers*. Kierkegaard owned a copy of the Greek text and also a translation by Børge Riisbrigh (Copenhagen: 1812). In this translation (I.5) there is the story that Pythagoras was the first to use the word *philosopher*. Doubt has been thrown by some scholars on this report. Just who did use the word *philosopher* first is of no significance for Kierkegaard's development of the analogy. See X¹ A 646 and X³ A 204 pp. 89-90, 101 above.

15. "For the use of the Dauphin," the eldest son of the French king. More particularly the phrase refers to an expurgated edition of Latin classics. By this expression Kierkegaard means that he will use a simple example. More pedagogically, however, the expression is an instance of Kierkegaard's way of halting a reader and prompting him to ask repeatedly, "What does this mean? What does the writer mean?"

16. Kierkegaard has reference here to the passage in Plato's *Phaedrus* (229d-230a) where Socrates, who had been occupied throughout his life with the question of self-knowledge, says he does not know whether he is a *Typhon* or "a monster more complicated and more furious than Typhon or a gentler and simpler creature to whom a divine and quiet lot is given by nature."

AN OPEN LETTER PROMPTED BY
A REFERENCE TO ME BY DR. RUDELBACH

1. See Introduction, pp. 30-31, for information concerning Dr. A. G. Rudelbach.

2. On Kierkegaard's two-track authorship see Introduction, and also "A Glance at a Contemporary Effort in Danish Literature" and "A First and Last Declaration" in *Concluding Unscientific Postscript*, pp. 225-66 and 551-54.

3. Throughout his life Kierkegaard steadfastly stayed clear of party affiliations of all kinds. Here the reference is particularly to the Grundt-vigians, with whom Rudelbach was associated. The primary basis of Kierkegaard's aversion to parties and cliques was his emphasis upon the authentic single individual in the context of the universally human and upon Christianity as addressed to every man.

4. Georg Frederik Ursin, *Regnebog eller Anviisning hensigtsmæssigen at udføre Huus- og Handelsregning* (Copenhagen: 1824). On the over-leaf of the title-page one dollar is promised for the first reporting of an incorrect answer. The book was published when Kierkegaard was in his fourth year of school.

5. In Greek mythology Tantalus was a Phrygian king who for his crimes was punished by confinement in water which receded when he tried to drink and near a tree bearing the finest fruit which always eluded his grasp—thence the word "tantalize." Here the phrase has a more direct reference to any situation or activity with unfulfilled and unfulfillable promises.

6. Acts 5:29.

7. Not asking leave of anybody.

SELECTED ENTRIES FROM THE JOURNALS AND PAPERS

1. Literally "shut-up-ness within oneself," but as a translation this is too awkward, although "reserve" or "reticence" is too weak.

2. Regine Olsen, to whom Kierkegaard was engaged from September 10, 1840, until October 11, 1841, when he broke the engagement primarily because of the burden of his melancholy and his singular sense of vocation. In May of 1843 she became engaged to Fridrich Schlegel and they were married November 3, 1847. See, for example, VIII^1 A 650.

3. For years Kierkegaard read Luther regularly, particularly his *En christelig Postille (Christian Sermons)*, I-II, tr. Jørgen Thisted (Copenhagen: 1828). This work is a collection of sermons on texts of the Church Year and is intended primarily for reading at home.

4. See Matthew 9:2 ff.

5. Having sold the house at Nytorv 2 in Copenhagen in December, 1847, Kierkegaard had taken a lease on rooms at Tornebuskegade 152 for April occupancy. Anders W. Christensen, Kierkegaard's house-man, had been conscripted by the military. "The difficulties of the times" refers to war with Germany, beginning March 8, 1848, and political unrest in Denmark, all of which resulted in a general financial crisis, in which Kierkegaard lost a considerable part of the house money invested in royal bonds.

6. The existential paradox of faith and forgiveness is that where humanly there is impossibility, there is nevertheless possibility in God. Therefore the chain of time is broken and time is caught up in divine possibility. Ethically man's impossibility is broken by releasing, redemptive forgiveness which transcends the ethical. Thus the life of faith is "immediacy or spontaneity after reflection." See, for example, *Fear and Trembling*, p. 108. See also VIII^1 A 681 and IX A 311.

7. This entry was written while Kierkegaard was working on *The Sickness unto Death*, published July 30, 1849. For his compact, at first bewildering, and penetrating characterization of spirit, see the opening two pages following the introduction. Although the present English translation is misleading at crucial points and compounds the difficulties inherent in the question and in the compactness of the formulation, these two pages of *The Sickness unto Death* are worth the ten or more

reflective readings required. They certainly are not a kind of Hegelian joke, as one writer has stated. See note 21, this chapter (to IX A 293).

8. See VIII¹ A 649 and note 6 above. For Kierkegaard the leap means qualitative discontinuity: bestowed innocence where there is guilt, release where there is bondage, possibility where there is impossibility, spontaneity where spontaneity has died.

9. A. G. Rudelbach, *Christelig Biographie*, I (Copenhagen: 1848). Kierkegaard owned and appreciated this work by Rudelbach. Two volumes had been announced but only one appeared.

10. Later spelled Anti-Climacus. For Kierkegaard, Johannes Climacus, the author of *Philosophical Fragments* (1844) and *Concluding Unscientific Postscript* (1846), represented the climax and the end (as seen at the time) of the pseudonymous writings as well as a level already transcended by Kierkegaard himself. Anti-Climacus and his books, *The Sickness unto Death* (1849) and *Training in Christianity* (1850), are not "against Climacus" but above Climacus and his books in ideality of presentation, and also above Kierkegaard. Irony and humor are abundantly present but are hardly dominant.

11. Kierkegaard had repeatedly characterized his work and himself as poetic—ideality and possibility in the medium of imagination. Professors as such are poetic in this sense also. Christianity, however, is a call to actuality in action and personal existence—imitation. Kierkegaard's personal battle at this time, during which the journal entries on imitating became numerous, centered on the question of becoming in act "as polemical" as that which he had presented in his writings. In the journals, the medieval term *imitatio* and the Danish *Efterfølgelse* (as in *The Imitation of Christ*) are criticized and cleansed, and the meaning as then defined is best carried by the English word *imitation* in spite of obvious imprecision and possible misunderstanding.

12. See *The Point of View for My Work as an Author* (posthumously published in 1859) for Kierkegaard's characterization of his entire authorship.

13. Here "non-reduplicated" means "direct" as contrasted to indirect communication or the mode of double-reflection, as in the pseudonymous works, which are works of reflection intended to occasion a second reflection—the reader's. For Kierkegaard "reduplication" usually means "existing in what one understands." But here "non-reduplicated" refers to

a mode of written expression; Kierkegaard was also wrestling with the suitability of direct written expression versus action as the appropriate direct expression. See, for example, IX B 64, pp. 77-79 above.

14. *The Crisis and a Crisis in the Life of an Actress*, by Inter et Inter (*Fædrelandet*, Nos. 188-91, July 24-27, 1848). This little article was the last of the works in the "esthetic" or indirect line in the double-tracked authorship of works under pseudonyms and works under his own name. After this there came works under the pseudonyms H. H. and Anti-Climacus, but they are direct nevertheless.

15. As far back as 1837 and earlier Kierkegaard had the idea that he would not live long, would not even outlive his father, who died August 9, 1839. Hence the title of Kierkegaard's first publication, *From the Papers of One Still Living*, September 7, 1838.

16. If this thought might have been a "gloomy notion," the thought of dying one's own death was of great importance to him (and related to his amazing productivity) and also to later existentialism.

17. Rasmus Nielsen was named Professor Extraordinarius in Moral Philosophy, University of Copenhagen, in 1841 and regular Professor of Philosophy in 1850. In 1848 there was the possibility that Professor Nielsen and Kierkegaard would become intimate enough so that Kierkegaard would have one "follower," but, consistent with his Socratic mode of ironical distance and his belief in the primacy of each individual in essential things, and also because of Nielsen's imperceptivity, he later diverted this exceptional relationship. See IX A 228 (pp. 71-72), 229-31.

18. See, for example, *Training in Christianity*, pp. 96 ff. and 127 ff., concerning direct communication and indirect communication in a work from this period (1848-50).

19. *Edifying Discourses in Various Spirits* (March 13, 1847), *Works of Love* (September 29, 1847), and *Christian Discourses* (April 26, 1848).

20. See note 14, this chapter, and IX A 218.

21. The Danish word "Aand" is more capacious than either "mind" or "spirit" as generally used in English. The two words, therefore, are employed together with a singular verb. Here Kierkegaard uses *Aand* and *Legeme* in the elemental sense of psycho-somatic. In *The Sickness unto Death* and in VIII[1] A 673 (p. 65 above), for example, *Aand* or *spirit* is the intended possibility for every man. See note 7, this chapter.

22. *The Point of View for My Work as an Author*.

23. See "Two Notes (published together with *The Point of View for My Work as an Author*), and section entitled INDIVIDUAL in *Søren Kierkegaard's Journals and Papers*, II (in process).

24. *A Cycle of Ethical-Religious Essays* had been planned and written. These were (1) "Something about What Could be Called Premise Authors," (2) "The Dialectical Relationship; the Universal, the Single Individual, the Special Individual," (3) "Has a Man the Right to Let Himself Be Put to Death for the Truth?" (4) "A Revelation in the Present Situation," (5) "The Catastrophe in Magister Adler's Life," and (6) "Of the Difference Between a Genius and an Apostle." Numbers 3 and 6 were published under the pseudonym H. H. on May 19, 1849. Here the three referred to are numbers 1, 2, and 4.

25. See X^1 A 422, (3) in par. 1, p. 84 above.

26. *The Sickness unto Death* and *Training in Christianity*.

27. A. G. Rudelbach, *Den evangeliske Kirkeforfatnings Oprindelse og Princip, dens Udartning og dens mulige Gjenrejsning fornemmelig i Danmark* (Copenhagen: 1849). See next entry, XX^1 A 669.

28. "The Accounting" is the major portion of a small work (which also includes "My Position as a Religious Writer in 'Christendom' and My Tactic") entitled *On My Work as an Author*, dated March, 1849, and published in 1851. In English translation it has been included with *The Point of View for My Work as an Author* (pp. 145-55).

29. See IX A 9, p. 66 above, X^1 A 510, p. 88 above, and note 10, this chapter.

30. See Matthew 27:43.

31. See Mark 9:49..

32. This reference and the entire paragraph allude to M. P. Kierkegaard, Søren Kierkegaard's father, who was the greatest single personal influence upon Kierkegaard's life. See *Works of Love*, Chapter IX, pp. 317 ff., and dedications to many of the edifying discourses.

33. See note 28, this chapter, and X^5 B 205, pp. 91-93 above.

34. See, for example, *Fear and Trembling*, pp. 78-80.

35. Niels Møller Spandet (1788-1858) was a judge and politician who was acquainted with N. F. S. Grundtvig as early as 1811 and remained closely allied to him and his work. In 1850 he proposed in parliament a law regarding Church affairs.

36. See note 27, this chapter (to X^1 A 660, p. 90 above).

37. *Training in Christianity*, pp. 139 ff.

38. *An Open Letter.*

39. See *Concluding Unscientific Postscript*, p. 175.

40. See *Philosophical Fragments,* p. 7.

41. See note 28, this chapter (to X⁵ B 205, pp. 91-93 above).

42. Anti-Climacus, pseudonymous author of *Training in Christianity*, published September 27, 1850.

43. J. P. Mynster, *Yderligere Bidrag til Forhandlingerne om de kirkelige Forhold i Danmark* (Copenhagen: 1851).

44. M. Goldschmidt, earlier the editor of *The Corsair*, a journal of anonymous gossip and political satire. He was challenged in an open letter, December 27, 1845, by Kierkegaard writing as Frater Taciturnus (see *Stages on Life's Way*, pp. 179 ff.), because he was the only Danish writer "who is not abused there." In 1846, after an outrageous personal attack on Kierkegaard in *The Corsair*, Goldschmidt, "accused" and "crushed" by the ideality of Kierkegaard's nature (M. Goldschmidt, *Livs Erindringer og Resultater*, Copenhagen: 1865, I, pp. 223-24), left *The Corsair*. Upon his return from Germany and Italy he founded *Nord og Syd* (December, 1847), a journal of quite different character.

45. Johannes Climacus, in *Concluding Unscientific Postscript*, p. 545.

46. This entry is a marginal addition to X⁴ A 604, entitled "Mynster." Reference is made to Kierkegaard's having spoken to Mynster about an appointment to the theological seminary. Kierkegaard ends the entry with the question whether he should work intensively (as he had done) or extensively (in a teaching position) and concludes that he must continue intensively and that in this Mynster himself, because he does not acknowledge Kierkegaard's request, has a responsibility.

COMMENTARY ON
ARMED NEUTRALITY AND *AN OPEN LETTER*

1. *Training in Christianity*, pp. 7, 211.

2. In 1851 Kierkegaard again urged "admission" in the following words: "And then, though a sting of the truth is contained in the propositions, everything nevertheless is made as lenient as possible, seeing that there is talk only of admissions and concessions, and indeed only of such concessions and admissions as everyone is left free to make for himself

before God" ("Supplement," *On My Work as an Author,* in *The Point of View,* p. 161).

3. X¹ A 74, p. 83 above.

4. X¹ A 116.

5. *Training in Christianity,* pp. 124-25; see also *Søren Kierkegaard's Journals and Papers,* I, Nos. 322 and 330.

6. VIII¹ A 649, p. 62 above.

7. X¹ A 360.

8. IV A 62.

9. It is worth noting that while working on "My Position as a Religious Writer in 'Christendom' and My Tactics" (the "Supplement" mentioned in note 2 above) Kierkegaard warns strongly against using his writings for the purpose of judging others. Among other things he says: "[I am] leaving it to each one just how he will make use of these productions—but in no case is anyone to use them for judging that others are not true Christians rather than for judging himself; for in that case I intend, if the opportunity is given, to take the part of those attacked, and if I am prevented and this does not happen, this is nevertheless what I would do" (X⁵ B 291:17).

10. *Works of Love,* pp. 121 ff.; 177 ff.

11. Included in *The Present Age.*

12. For example, see X¹ A 551 and other entries on this theme under MARTYRDOM in *Søren Kierkegaard's Journals and Papers,* III (in preparation).

13. X³ A 576. See also IX A 148 and IX A 226 and compare X¹ A 646 (pp. 89-90 above) and X² A 640.

14. See *Concluding Unscientific Postscript,* p. 553, and IX A 68.

15. When with reference to his work Kierkegaard uses the term "reformation" once and only once in *Armed Neutrality* (p. 38 above), he is thinking only of the subjective, existential change in the single individual, which was the aim of his activity as an author.

16. *Om det borgerlige Ægteskab,* p. 4.

17. Ibid., p. 70.

18. *Armed Neutrality,* p. 41 above.

19. The idea of martyrdom as the highest way for the Christian is accented even more strongly in Kierkegaard's draft of the open letter against Rudelbach. See X⁵ B 124, pp. 105-6 above.

20. A play on the word *Christendom* (Christianity) and *Christen*

(Christian) plus *dum* (stupid, dense, dumb). In this word, which he himself coined, Kierkegaard indicates the true Christian's simplicity and disinterestedness toward external organization.

21. See note 27, p. 168 above.

22. X⁴ A 20, p. 104 above.

23. X⁴ A 38.

24. *Fædrelandet*, No. 38, February 14, 1851.

25. X⁴ A 100.

26. XI² A 334. In 1839 Grundtvig became pastor at Vartov in Copenhagen; from 1848 Rudelbach was pastor of St. Mikkels in Slagelse.

GUIDE TO

"SELECTED ENTRIES"

Pages on which they appear in the present volume.

INDEX

ABOUT THE EDITORS

Howard V. Hong, Professor of Philosophy at St. Olaf College, is widely known for his translations of other works by Kierkegaard, including the *Philosophical Fragments*, *Works of Love*, and *Søren Kierkegaard's Journals and Papers*. Edna H. Hong, co-editor of *Journals and Papers*, is author of *Muskego Boy* and *Clues to the Kingdom*. Gregor Malantschuk is Kierkegaard Research Fellow at the University of Copenhagen.